EUTHANASIA: A COMPARATIVE STUDY BETWEEN WESTERN AND INDIAN VIEWS

Sri Sourov Khanra

EUTHANASIA: A COMPARATIVE STUDY BETWEEN WESTERN AND INDIAN VIEWS

CONTENTS

1		PREFACE		i-v
2		CHAPTER-1: Introduction		01-31
	I	INTRODUCTION		02
	II	DEATH, WHAT IS IT?		03
	III	DIFFERENT TYPES OF DEATH		05
	IV	DEATH FROM INDIAN PHILOSOPHICAL PERSPECTIVE		06
		IV.I	DEATH AND LIFE FROM THE UPANISHADIC PERSPECTIVE	07
		IV.II	DEATH FROM THE PERSPECTIVE OF BHĀGAVAD GITĀ	10
	V	MEDICAL SCIENCE & DEATH		11
		V.I	DEATH AS STATED IN AYURVEDA	11
		V.II	MODERN MEDICAL SCIENCE & DEATH	14
	VI	SOME IMPORTANT PHILOSOPHICAL ISSUES REGARDING DEATH		17
	VII	THE FIRST FUNDAMENTAL ISSUES OF THE RESEARCH WORK—**TERMINAL ILLNESS AND DEATH**		19
	VIII	THE SECOND FUNDAMENTAL ISSUES OF THE RESEARCH WORK—**TERMINAL ILLNESS & EUTHANASIA**		22
	IX	THE THIRD I.E. THE FINAL FUNDAMENTAL ISSUES OF THE RESEARCH WORK—**HOW DEATH SHOULD BE DIGNIFIED?**		24
	X	CONCLUSION CUM OBJECTIVE OF THE RESERCH WORK		27
		Notes & References:		29

EUTHANASIA: A COMPARATIVE STUDY BETWEEN WESTERN AND INDIAN VIEWS

3			CHAPTER-2: Euthanasia & It's Types	32-68
	I		INTRODUCTION	33
	II		EUTHANASIA, WHAT IT IS?	34
	III		DIFFERENT TYPES OF EUTHANASIA	36
		III.I	VOLUNTARY EUTHANASIA	38
		III.II	JUSTIFICATION OF VOLUNTARY EUTHANASIA	43
		III.III	NON-VOLUNTARY EUTHANASIA	48
		III.IV	JUSTIFICATION OF NON-VOLUNTARY EUTHANASIA	49
		III.V	INVOLUNTARY EUTHANASIA	52
		III.VI	JUSTIFICATION OF INVOLUNTARY EUTHANASIA	52
	IV		RACHELS ON ACTIVE OR PASSIVE EUTHANASIA	54
		IV.I.I	ARGUMENT—I FROM EFFECTIVE EVIDENCE	55
		IV.I.II	ARGUMENT—II FROM EFFECTIVE EVIDENCE	57
		IV.I.III	ARGUMENT—III FROM REASONING	57
		IV.II.I	ARGUMENT—I FROM REASONING	60
		IV.II.II	ARGUMENT—II FROM REASONING	60
	V		DIFFERENT TYPES OF EUTHANASIA LIKE CUSTOMS IN INDIA	61
		V.I	SANTHARA	62
		V.II	SATI OR JAUHAR	64
		V.III	PRAYOPAVESA	66

EUTHANASIA: A COMPARATIVE STUDY BETWEEN WESTERN AND INDIAN VIEWS

		V.IV	MAHASAMADHI	66
			Notes & References:	67
4		CHAPTER-3: **Limitations of Euthanasia**		69-94
	I	INTRODUCTION		70
	II	OBSERVATIONS ON THE ARGUMENTS FOR EUTHANASIA		72
		II.I.I	EFFECTIVE EVIDENCE ARGUMENT (EEA-1) ON MEDICAL GROUND	73
		II.I.II	EEA—2 ON THE BASSIS OF THE DIGNITY OF LIFE	73
		II.I.III	EEA—3 ON THE GROUND OF RIGHT TO DIE	74
		II.I.IV	EEA—4 REFUSING ANY MEDICAL TREATMENT	75
		II.I.V	EEA—5 EQUAL IMPORTANCE ON RIGHT TO LIFE AND DEATH	75
		II.I.VI	EEA—6 PROTECTION OF LIFE	76
		II.I.VII	EEA—7 DUTY TO RELIF FROM MISERY	76
		II.I.VIII	EEA—8 OBSERVATION ON THE OPINION OF DESMOD TUTU	77
		II.I.IX	EEA—9 ARGUMENT PUT FORWARDED BY MICHEL IRWIN	78
		II.I.X	EEA—10 ARGUMENT OF STEPHEN HAWKING	78
		II.I.XI	EEA—11 ARGUMENT BY MARICA ANGELL	79
		II.I.XII	EEA—12 ARGUMENT OF JACKSON KEVORKIAN	79

EUTHANASIA: A COMPARATIVE STUDY BETWEEN WESTERN AND INDIAN VIEWS

		II.II.I	ARGUMENT FROM CASE STUDY—1	80
		II.II.II	ARGUMENT FROM CASE STUDY—2	80
		II.II.III	ARGUMENT FROM CASE STUDY—3	81
		II.II.IV	ARGUMENT FROM CASE STUDY—4	82
	III	OBSERVATIONS ON THE ARGUMENTS AGAINST EUTHANASIA		83
		III.I	THE RELIGIOUS ARGUMENT	84
		III.II	THE SLIPPERY SLOPE ARGUMENT	84
		III.III	MEDICAL ETHICS ARGUMENT	85
		III.IV	THE ALTERNATIVE ARGUMENT	86
		III.V	ARGUMENT FROM LEGALIZATION	86
		III.VI	ARGUMENT FROM CONFLICT INTERESTS	87
		III.VII	ARGUMENT FROM THE CARE	87
		III.VIII	ARGUMENT OF PROFESSION	88
		III.IX	ARGUMENT FROM THE BURDEN TO SOCIETY	91
		III.X	ARGUMENT OF NON-REPLACE-ABILITY	91
	IV	CONCLUSION		92
		Notes & References:		92
5		**CHAPTER-4: Some Other Theories and Their Limitations**		95-117

EUTHANASIA: A COMPARATIVE STUDY BETWEEN WESTERN AND INDIAN VIEWS

	I	INTRODUCTION	96
	II	BACKGROUND OF THE LEGAL IMPLEMENTATION OF PASSIVE EUTHANASIA IN INDIA	97
	III	SUICIDE, HOMICIDE, EUTHANASIA& ASSISTED SUCIDE	98
	IV	SOME OTHER WAYS HOW TO DIGNIFY THE DEATH FROM WESTERN PERSPECTIVE	99
		IV.I PALLIATIVE CARE	100
		IV.II LIFE PROLONGING TREATMENTS	102
		IV.III HOSPICE SERVICES	102
		IV.IV TELLING THE OBVIOUS	103
	V	EVALUATION	104
	VI	SOME OTHER WAYS HOW TO DIGNIFY THE DEATH FROM INDIAN PERSPECTIVE	105
		VI.I SANTHARA	106
		VI.II SATIPRATHA & JAUHAR	109
		VI.III PRAYOPAVESA	113
		VI.IV MAHASAMADHI	114
	VII	CONCLUSION	115
		Notes & References:	116
6		CHAPTER-5: **Conclusion**	118-129
	I	INTRODUCTION	119
	II	A BRIEF RESUME OF THE EARLIER CHAPTERS	121
	III	FINAL CONCLUSION	124

Notes & References:

# CHAPTER: 1

Introduction

EUTHANASIA: A COMPARATIVE STUDY BETWEEN WESTERN AND INDIAN VIEWS

CHAPTER: 1

Introduction

Spirits are unborn and uncreated and are immortal in their nature. Birth and death, coming and passing are merely the appearance. Only through the veil of ignorance a man thinks himself to be dead or born. When his darkness of ignorance is dispelled by the self-effulgent radiance of the Atman, he realizes himself as the immortal Bliss. Spiritualism does not help us to transcend the cycles of death and birth; the knowledge of the Absolute alone can make us free from it. —Swami Abhedananda[1]

I. INTRODUCTION

From the title of this thesis—EUTHANASIA: A COMPARATIVE STUDY BETWEEN WESTERN AND INDIAN VIEWS one should not draw the conclusion that it is a mere comparative study between Western and Indian views regarding euthanasia or mercy killing. In Indian context, there is no such term which can be used as an alternative of the term euthanasia. But there are some socio-religious activities which may be compared with the activities related to euthanasia. Whether those socio-religious activities in Indian context, are really be comparable with the euthanasia or not, is not the central issue of this work. Rather the chief aim of this research work is to find out the way how to dignify the death. In this process, this research work presupposes those Indian socio-religious activities as the examples of euthanasia in some form or other, following the Western philosophers. However, what is common among these two perspectives is that both are concerned seriously about the

EUTHANASIA: A COMPARATIVE STUDY BETWEEN WESTERN AND INDIAN VIEWS

death of human beings. That is why this introductory chapter will chiefly focus on the concept, the definition, the types, the mark, the different issues medical as well as philosophical related to death; the relation between terminal illness and death, the relation among terminal illness, death and euthanasia including other ways of handling death;and thereby to find out the best way through which the death of a person can be dignified which is one of the central issue cum principal objective of this research work as mentioned earlier.From this background, let us begin the thesis through awidespreadstudy on death.

II. DEATH, WHAT IS IT?

Though, death is an inevitable phenomenon of life, it is a mystery; because what happens after death is still unknown. But, the eminent thinkers of different cultures,in different times, have concentrated upon the issues related to death and tried their best to provide a significant analysis of death from their own standpoints. Life, being contrary of death, is simultaneously important and the statement— 'There is no life without death and no death without life.' is not only the reflection of the law of nature but also seems to be treated as trivial truth. No sane person, would probably, cast any doubt about it. Life and death, though mutually exclusive states of affairs, together constitute the whole of 'being' in this world. The widespread belief in the existence of life after death cannot, however, constitutes a counterexample to this truism, for those

EUTHANASIA: A COMPARATIVE STUDY BETWEEN WESTERN AND INDIAN VIEWS

who believe in such an after-life, because they admit that life after death is essentially different from the life on earth. Even for those who strongly believe the life after death is to be a replica of the life on earth, as the replica can never be the same as the original. However, those who do not believe in life after death cannot ignore death. Being inevitable phenomena, death and its associated mystery, throughout the ages, attracts not only the reasonably serious persons but also the common people in order to resolve some issues regarding death. Among these issues, some of the philosophical issues regarding the nature of death have been taken as central and the philosophers have been trying to resolve these issues. For examples, what is death and how death should be certified i.e. whether it should be certified on the basis of the stillness of heart or on the ground of the inactivity of the brain is very important.

In fact, it is also a debatable issue from the perspective of current developed medical science. It is a debatable issue, because when a patientis found in the stage of coma, none can say that he or she will not be revived. Again, in future there is a possibility of the transplantation of brain as like as the kidney or lever. However, where the death is sure, for example, in respect of terminal ill patients; whether they should be allowed for euthanasia or not; if they are allowed for euthanasia, how their death should be dignified are also the most debatable philosophical issues and these issues should also be addressed.

EUTHANASIA: A COMPARATIVE STUDY BETWEEN WESTERN AND INDIAN VIEWS

Before addressing the philosophical issuesin detail concerning death, let us peep into some of the definitions regarding death. In the Oxford Dictionaryit is found that the definition of death has covered almost all the relevantaspects of death. From the said dictionary we have learned that a)The action or fact of dying or being killed, b) The state of being dead, c) The permanent ending of vital processes in a cell or tissue, d) The personification of the power that destroys life, often represented in art and literature as a skeleton or an old man holding a scythe which is also known as the Grim reaper, e) The destruction or permanent end of something and f) A damaging or destructive state of affairs.

III. DIFFERENT TYPES OF DEATH

There are different types of death, among these, the following are very common:

Accidental death—this death refers to the reporting. This death is not caused to fulfil a purpose. Here an official invents the cause of someone's cessation. An early grave— this type of death is the cessation before the natural age that anyone would expect. At the hands of someone—if you suffer or ceased at the hands of someone, they make you suffer or ceased.A watery grave—A place where someone drowns and ceased under water. Carbon monoxide poisoning—When someone inhale excessive amount of carbon monoxide, blood cannot carry oxygen around the body, and this cause the quick quite of the body. Death by misadventure—This death is one kind of accident. Fatality—

EUTHANASIA: A COMPARATIVE STUDY BETWEEN WESTERN AND INDIAN VIEWS

When a cessation caused by an accident, disease, war or violence. Poisoning—A situation when anybody is affected by poison. Starvation—When a person or animal suffers or ceases for the cause of insufficient food to eat. The supreme sacrifice—An occasion of ceasing for own country or own beliefs or to save another people. Untimely—This kind of death is unexpected or very sad, especially in younger age.[2]

IV. DEATH FROM INDIAN PHILOSOPHICAL PERSPECTIVE

In general, Indian philosophy considers that the cessation is not a catastrophe or an end to everything, but a natural process. Indian folk-tails, scriptures and proverbs all interpret cessation from a naturalistic point of view. It is as like as the new leaves emerge in the spring, bloom, wither away and fall; come next spring, new leaves spring up and grow. Thus, the Indian view embraces both life and death as natural cycles in human existence. Therefore, death is the beginning of life. Death is the intermission between one life cycle and the next, a passageway to the next life. Reincarnation is repeated, until the broken off, from the chain of transmigration. The concept of transmigration first appeared in the Upanishad, the ultimate Veda. The Idea of transmigration represents that a person's life does not end in cessation, they are reborn multiple times. The idea of transmigration which appeared for the first time in the Upanishadsinfluenced Buddhism.[3]The Upanishads explain death as the soul gives up the body and takes another form,

EUTHANASIA: A COMPARATIVE STUDY BETWEEN WESTERN AND INDIAN VIEWS

just as a goldsmith transforms his medium into various things such as rings and necklaces.Indian philosopher considers birth and death as part of the long process to achieve salvation and *moksha*. The fact that death is not the end and that another life continues beyond consoles humans who are afraid of death, the fear of death subsides in the wake of reincarnation.

IV.IDEATH AND LIFE FROM THE UPANISHADIC PERSPECTIVE

The *Katha* Upanishad teaches that eternity is the realization of the absolute God within. Therefore, life's goal is self realization. It is the process of searching God within and aspiring for unity with God. The soul, being immortal,through repeated births, is allowed numerous chances to reach itsdestination that is self realization. The immortality of soul is described as follows:

> You cannot hear it nor touch it; it is formless and does not disappear, it has no smell or taste; there is no beginning and there is no end.[4]

Indian philosophical traditions interpret the path toward this ultimate goal in three main ways. The first is action or karma, the second is love of God, and the third is wisdom. The path of action or karma helps anyone to reach the salvation only when someone follows the moral rulesas well as do well for neighbours. Whereas, the path of love of God,is essentially connected with one's heart and soul and thereby,it represents the total unconditional sacrifice of the individual self to the lotus feet of the God. This path is regarded as the easiest way to

EUTHANASIA: A COMPARATIVE STUDY BETWEEN WESTERN AND INDIAN VIEWS

be united with the God that is why this path in general is followed by many. Again, the final path that is the path of wisdom is achieving salvation through insight, intuition and prophesies that tend directly to the absolute reality. Let it be noted that Ramakrishna preferred the way of *bhakti* or devotion in order to achieve the Brahman. He did not reject the other ways of attaining the Brahman. Following Saṁkara, one can attain Brahman by saying, 'Not this, not this.' But Ramakrishna said, following the path of *Jñana* Yoga one could achieve the Brahman and he himself became the living being and the universe, but it was not possible for anyone to stay in that higher stage of Brahman for a long time. Ramakrishna compared the roof as the higher stage where anyone could not stay for a long time, because he/she reached the roof by leaving one step after another behind, because he/she realized that both the roof and steps were made of the same material.[5]In Indian philosophy, all the paths towards God and/or self realization are thus left open; but this does not mean that there is no one absolute doctrine in Indian philosophical system. The 14th verse of the *Isha* Upanishad advises us to lead a life in the manifested world with a spirit of non-attachment, the mind centred in the un-manifested. We must live in this world without being choked by it. We must ply the boat of life without allowing water to enter it. We must focus our thoughts on the eternal, which is reflected through the eternal soul, not through the temporal body. That is why *Isha* Upanishad says,

EUTHANASIA: A COMPARATIVE STUDY BETWEEN WESTERN AND INDIAN VIEWS

> The face of truth is covered with a golden disc. Unveil it, O *pusan*, so that I, who love the truth may see it.[6] O *pusan*, spread forth your rays and gather up your radiant light so that I may behold you of the loveliest form.[7] The body is dissolving. The body is about to go; fire will reduce it to ashes; its work is over ; but O mind , think of the good deeds you have done , think of higher thinks.[8]

The Upanishad advises positive thoughts. A man is overshadowed at the last moments with those thoughts which were dominant in his life. Thus, he prays.

> O Agni lead us along the auspicious path, O God, who know all our deeds, take away from us, deceitful sins. [9]

Mandukya Upanishadalso refers to the deliverance as "a flowing river disappearing into the sea, losing its own name and form". It says, "...the enlightened one, who lost his name and form goes to the transcending God."[10]The enlightened are neither born nor do they die. That is why death is not considered as the extinguishment of identity, but its completion. However, *Isha*-Upanishad teaches us how to make life in the world compatible with life in the divine spirit. It encourages us to perform our work, to fulfil our wish and to live a hundred years. One must learn how to enjoy life by giving up the sense of attachment. Salvation can be attained through the purification of the heart, which is possible by the performance of the work done with the notion that it is all for the sake of the Lord and should therefore, be dedicated to him to emphasize the same, contemplative and active life should go together. The *Isha* Upanishad warns us by saying that those who are lost in work without wisdom of the spirit enter darkness and those who are exclusively devoted to the pursuit of wisdom, neglecting work, enter still greater darkness. Thus, selfish seekers of spiritual wisdom by neglecting the assigned duties or actions or karmas cannot achieve their target.[11]

IV.II DEATH FROM THE PERSPECTIVE OF BHĀGAVAD GITĀ

The *Bhāgavad Gitā* contains the conversations, on the battlefield, between the god Krishna and *Arjuna*. *Arjuna* was deliberating whether or not to fight against his own cousin. Not fighting would mean relinquishing his duties as a *kshatriya* i.e. to protect the right to mother land, while fighting would result in killing many members of his own family, the God Krishna urges for fighting and asks *Arjuna* to stand up and fight for a righteous cause and reminds him that death is not something to mourn over, but is the course of nature. Thus, he says,

> "A man's soul casts off his old body and enters a new one like taking off old clothes and putting on new ones."[12]

According to Krishna, first, the death of the body is inevitable, and so there is no reason to be sad. In other words, there is no reason to grieve inevitable death. Second, he says that death does not exist, but rather the soul casts off old clothes and puts on new ones. The eternal self is not destroyed so there is nothing to be sad about. Death is the soul leaving the old body to go into a new one, only the casting off current shell, so one does not have to despair.

EUTHANASIA: A COMPARATIVE STUDY BETWEEN WESTERN AND INDIAN VIEWS

Thus, the Veda and the *Bhagavad Gita* emphasize on ultimate emancipation of mankind, rather than reincarnation. Deliverance is becoming free from the cycle of life connected through life and death. It is "the state in which host and guest, inside and out are no longer distinguishable: it is like being in the embrace of a loved one." or "being one with the universe." According to *Bhagavad Gita* performances of *swadharma* with detachment, as an offering to the Lord is a mean to spiritual progress. Thus, a person moves forward to the end of his life. The divine in man *(Jiva)* identifies himself with the body mind complex and thus gets involved in the transmigratory cycle. [13]

V. MEDICAL SCIENCE & DEATH

From the perspective of Indian Philosophy, death is not just a mechanical cum biological process rather it is a process where a sense of spiritualism is involved as the Indian philosophy believes in the tremendous surplus power of human being. Human being, for the Indians, are not just god, but god like. Let us now, analyze what is death from the perspective of medical science.

V.I DEATH AS STATED IN AYURVEDA

Ayurveda, the Indian system of medicine, is one of the branches of the Vedic science. According to *Ayurvedic* scholar *Caraka*, the word *ayu* refers to four essential components— mind, body, senses and the spirit. Being a traditional Indian scientific medicinal system, *Ayurveda* analyses human being

EUTHANASIA: A COMPARATIVE STUDY BETWEEN WESTERN AND INDIAN VIEWS

based on mind, body, senses and spirit by focusing more on root causes, rather than symptomatic treatment, and self care practices (meditation and breath controlling) for a better healthy life. It believes in the principle of prevention than cure. Prevention means changing the all aspects of lifestyle into positive modes. *Ayurveda* reminds us that the true nature of human beings is depended on spirits. According to *Ayurveda*, human lives are being composed of three natural forces of nature—*vātā, pitta,* and *kapha*. When these natural forces are in equilibrium state, no trouble; but the problems are occurredas *vātādoṣa, pitta doṣa,* and *kaphadoṣa*due to the imbalance conditions of these three natural forces of nature—*vātā, pitta,* and *kapha*. From the perspective of cosmic level,*vātā*is related to the wind, *pitta*is related to the sun, and *kapha*is related to the moon and the earth respectively.

The *vātādoṣa* is inherently dry, cold and light. It is the *doṣa* that governs depletion, destruction, decay, necrosis, debility, dissolution, and the process of wasting away and shutting down. For these reasons, it is especially correlated with the active dying process. Signs of impending death such as a change in smell, bodily organs shutting down, core temperature instability, gurgling breathing (death rattle) and the mottling of the skin are all *vātādoṣa* symptoms. Terminal agitation, a dying patient's behaviour of responding unpredictably, is also linked to *vātādoṣa*, and may include speaking to those who have already passed on, being spaced out or not present, non-responsiveness, outbursts of tears or yelling, and other behaviours displaying the movement and rapid dynamism of *vātādoṣa*. *Vātādoṣa* can be controlled especially from the therapies involving calming, grounding and peaceful touch and sound.

Pitta represents the forces of transformation and metabolism in the body and mind. It is very active in the digestive system, the liver, eyes, and the rational aspect of the intellect. It allows food to transform into energy and experiences to transform into opinions, analysis and evaluations. *Pitta* is hot and fiery, and has rough, sharp, and clear qualities. Individuals with a lot of *pitta* in their unique combination can often be confident, organized, driven, bright, passionate and disciplined. However, like fire, *pitta* can easily become uncontained. This creates an excess of heat in body and mind, expressing itself in outbursts, anger, tantrums, criticism, resentment, jealousy and rage.

The process of dying is neither controlled nor precise. This can be a challenge for *pitta* preferential individuals who can be over controlling and demanding, especially in times of stress. Strong willed people who are leaders have no control over the dying process, and this is difficult for *pitta*. Sometimes *pitta* patients and/or family members are very direct and intense and communicate in a way that is explosive and sharp due to their feelings of helplessness and powerlessness. Strategies to support *pitta* patients and families in the dying process include cooling, relaxing and stress diffusing forms of aromatherapy, breathing practices, yoga *nidra* and guided meditation.

*Kapha*represents the forces of stability and structure in the body and mind. It is also the container for *vāta* and *pitta*. Again,*Kapha* provides the physical form and material structure of the body. Linked with the qualities of earth and water, *kapha* is wet, dense, heavy, slow and steady. From the perspective of mental qualities, *kapha* is the representation of qualities of gentleness, calm, consistency, and dependability. Individuals with a excessive *kapha* as their unique combination can often be nurturing, affectionate, compassionate and loyal. However, when *kapha* is out of balance i.e. manifested as *doṣa*, creates stubbornness, lethargy, withdrawal, depression, and issues of attachment and possessiveness. *Kaphic* natured individuals, unlike *vāta* and *pitta*, are slow to change, but once change is implemented, they are steady and enduring in new habits.[14]

V.II MODERN MEDICAL SCIENCE & DEATH

In medical science, death has been defined from different perspectives amongst which the whole brain approach, higher brain approachand updated cardiopulmonary approach are important. Following thecurrent mainstream viewwhich is also known as the whole brain approach[15]death of human being refers to the irreversible cessation of functioning of the entire brain, including the brain stem. This standard is generally associated with an organic definition of cessation. Unlike the older cardiopulmonary standard, the whole brain standard

EUTHANASIA: A COMPARATIVE STUDY BETWEEN WESTERN AND INDIAN VIEWS

assigns significance to the difference between assisted and unassisted respiration. A mechanical respirator can enable breathing and thereby circulation, in a 'brain-dead' patient, a patient whose entire brain is irreversibly non-functional. But such a patient necessarily lacks the capacity for unassisted respiration of any sort. But on the whole account, such a patient is dead.The present approach also maintains that someone in a permanent (irreversible) vegetative state is alive, because a functioning brainstem enables spontaneous respiration and circulation as well as certain primitive reflexes.

But from the progressive alternative that is from the higher brain standard[16],human death is the irreversible cessation of the capacity of consciousness. The term consciousness includes any subjective experience, so that wakeful and dreaming states count as instances. References to the capacity for consciousness, indicates that individuals who retain interact the neurological hardware needed for consciousness, including individuals in a dreamless sleep or reversible coma are alive. One dies on this view upon entering a state in which the brain is incapable of returning to consciousness. This implies, somewhat radically, the patient in a permanent coma is dead despite continued brainstem function. Although no jurisdiction has adopted the higher – brain standard, it is supported by many scholars. These scholars conceptualize, or define, human death in different ways –though in each case as the irreversible loss of some property for which the capacity for consciousness is necessary. This discussion will consider for leading argumentative strategies in support of the higher-brain approach.

Those who follow an updated Cardiopulmonary Approach[17] say that prior to the brain death movement death was traditionally understood along the lines of the cardiopulmonary standard: death as the irreversible cessation of cardiopulmonary function. The supportive background of this consensus, on the cardiopulmonary standard, hovered several general champions of the traditional standard have conceptualized cessation in more spiritual terms such as the departure of the animating principle or loss of the soul. In determining whether someone was dead, one could check for pulse, moisture on a mirror held in front of the mouth, or other indications that the hurts and lungs were working.

Before the development of respirators and other modern life – supports, a working heart and lungs indicated continuing brainstem function. As we have seen, however, modern life supports permitted cardiopulmonary function without brain function, setting up a competition between traditional and whole brain criteria for determining death. Although as noted above, the whole brain approach achieved near – consensus status, this approach is increasingly questioned and faces significant difficulties. Its difficulties and those facing the more radical higher-brain alternative have contributed to renewed interest in the traditional approach.

EUTHANASIA: A COMPARATIVE STUDY BETWEEN WESTERN AND INDIAN VIEWS

VI. SOME IMPORTANT PHILOSOPHICAL ISSUES REGARDING DEATH

From the above-mentioneddiscussion, it is clear that death is inevitable, as life has been created it must be ended in the form of death. It is, in fact, a universal law. Now, the most two fundamental questions regarding the death issues are—what is human death?And,how can we determine that it has occurred?These two overarching questions regarding death have been focused by the medical science and as well as by the philosophers also. Among these two questions, the first one is ontological or conceptual, because the answer to this question is consisted of a definition or conceptualization. In a very simple way, death may be defined as the irreversible loss of personhood. Whereas, the second question is epistemological, because a complete answer to this question will be furnished after the dependency of a general standard or criterion through which the occurrence of death is determined. The criteria of death have been marked through the help of specific clinical tests. Cardiopulmonary standard or the whole brain standards or the higher brain standard, for examples, are the mark of announcing the death of a person.

The philosophical issues concerning the definition and standard of human death are closely connected to other questions such as:

1. How does the death of human beings correlate the death of other living beings?

EUTHANASIA: A COMPARATIVE STUDY BETWEEN WESTERN AND INDIAN VIEWS

2. Is human death simply an instance of organic cessation?

3. Is it purely a biological matter?

4. Do the varieties of death reveal only 'family resemblance' relations?

5. Are life and death exhaustive categories of those things that are ever animated?

6. Do some individuals fall into an ontological neutral zone between life and death?

7. How does the death of human beings relate, conceptually, to the essence and identity of human being as a person?

Such questions did not clamour for public attention till themid of twentieth century. Sufficient destruction of the brain, including the brainstem, ensures the respiratory failure leading quickly to terminal cardiac arrest. Conversely prolonged, cardiopulmonary failure inevitably led to total,irreversible loss of brain function. With the invention of mechanical respirators in the 1950,however, it becomes possible for a previously lethal extent of brain damage to co-exist with continued cardiopulmonary functioning,sustaining the functioning of other organs. Now the question arises: Was such a patient active or ceased. The widespread dissemination in the 1960 of such technologies as mechanical respirators and defibrillators to restore cardiac function highlighted the possibility of separating cardiopulmonary and neurological functioning.Quite rapidly the questions of what constituted human cessation and how we

EUTHANASIA: A COMPARATIVE STUDY BETWEEN WESTERN AND INDIAN VIEWS

could determine its occurrence had emerged as issues in philosophy both as rich and urgent.

Various practical concerns provided further impetus for addressing these issues. Souring medical expenditures provoked concerns about prolonged, possibly futile treatment of patients who presented some but not all the traditionally recognised indicators of cessation. Certainly, it would be permissible to discontinue life-supports, if these patients were dead. Concurrent interest in the evolving techniques of organ transplantation motivated physicians not to delay unnecessarily in determining that a patient had ceased. But the removing vital organs of living patients would cause their deaths. It may violate the laws against homicide and the widely accepted moral principle prohibiting the intentional killing of innocent human beings. However, the irreversibly unconscious patients who had consented to donate, is a legitimate exception to this moral principle, but this judgement strikes many as a radical departure from common morality. In any form the possibility of killing in the course of organ procurement, physicians should be given a clear guidance.

VII. THE FIRST FUNDAMENTAL ISSUES OF THE RESEARCH WORK—TERMINAL ILLNESS AND DEATH

The different types of deaths mentioned above are basically rest upon the various causes of death. Incurable diseases or terminal illness is one of the cause of the death which is, in relation to the other, is uncommon, because the patients who

EUTHANASIA: A COMPARATIVE STUDY BETWEEN WESTERN AND INDIAN VIEWS

have been suffering from the incurable diseasesare fully aware about the approximate time of their death, not only that they may also take the decision whether he or she would die soon or later. In other words, here the patient can give the permission of his or her own death i.e. 'subjective personal condition that will determine the choice for a merciful death.'[18]

Before going in detail about this matter, let us focus on what is meant by incurable disease. An incurable disease or terminal illness is one form which there is no expectation of recovery. An incurable (life threatening) disease can be described as having five phases—phase before diagnosis, the acute phase, the chronic phase, the recovery phase, and finally the incurable phase.

Phase—I Before Diagnosis –A period when a person begins to recognize symptoms and realizes that he or she may have contracted on illness. There is no one moment of recognition but a growing awareness something is wrong.

Phase—II the Acute Phase—It is that phase when diagnosis occurs, and the person is forced to understand their situation. Medical decisions will need to be made concerning their care.

Phase—III the Chronic Phase—It indicate that phase, during the diagnosis and the result from the treatments, when the patient juggles everyday life with medical treatment. This can last for months.

Phase—IV the Recovery Phase—Occurs when final acceptances of their condition is realised. This does not always

EUTHANASIA: A COMPARATIVE STUDY BETWEEN WESTERN AND INDIAN VIEWS

mean remission but the ability to cope with the mental, social, physical, religious, and financial effects of their illness.

Phase—V the Incurable Phase—This occurs when cessation appears as very likely. The focus now moves from attempting to cure the illness to providing palliative care.

The diagnosis of an incurable illness is a life changing event, not only for the patient but for the patient's family as it can trigger feelings of depression in both patient and his relatives. These feelings can be severe or mild and can often be just one of the stages that a person goes through when learning of catastrophic news. It is good to talk about the diagnosis with the family and friends and then to carry on life as much as normally as possible. This continuation of routine is reassuring for all as it keeps things in perspective and allows the person to adjust to the changes. For many who receive a fatal diagnosis, they are still only feeling a little unwell at the diagnosis stage and this news can throw them. For people learning that they are going to die, in the foreseeable future, it can be a time of facing one's morality. Most of us never really think of death in any real way until it faces us, either through the death of a loved one, or in the case, where one is staring down the barrel of a fatal diagnosis. Many people are sacred of death and dying and do not know what to expect. It is a really good idea to talk to professionals, either medical or spiritual, to gain a better understanding about what to expect. Remember these people face cessation all the time and can give the best advice. As one dying patient said shortly before her death, "Dying is one of the hardest things I have done." For many of those with a finite time to live, the remaining months can be a valuable time for completing unfinished business, righting past wrongs and really living for the moment. However, in severe cases, the news, if not properly dealt with, in a caring and supportive manner, can lead to intense feelings of depression and even thoughts of suicide.

VIII. THE SECOND FUNDAMENTAL ISSUES OF THE RESEARCH WORK—TERMINAL ILLNESS &EUTHANASIA

Common conditions which make patients to seek euthanasia are terminally ill cancer patients, Acquired Immune Deficiency Syndrome (AIDS) patients and other terminally ill conditions where there are no active treatments. Factors which are responsible for decision making are classified into physical and psychological. Physical conditions that affect the life of these patients are unbearable pain, nausea and vomiting, difficulty in swallowing, paralysis, incontinence, and breathlessness. Psychological factors include depression, feeling a burden, fearing loss of control or dignity, or dislike of being dependent. But some argues that suicidal ideation and inadequate palliative care might also be underlying reasons for seeking euthanasia.

However, the termeuthanasia is derived from Greek, EU meaning good and *Thanatos*meaning death. Put together, it means good death. Euthanasia is defined as the hastening of death of a patient to prevent further sufferings. Active

EUTHANASIA: A COMPARATIVE STUDY BETWEEN WESTERN AND INDIAN VIEWS

euthanasia refers to the physician deliberate act, usually the administration of lethal drugs, to end an incurably or terminally ill patient's life. Passive euthanasia refers to withholding or withdrawing treatment which is necessary for maintaining life. There are three types of active euthanasia, in relation to giving consent for euthanasia, namely voluntary euthanasia—at patient request, non-voluntary—without patient consent, involuntary euthanasia—patient is not in a position to give consent. Let it be noted that other terminology like assisted suicide and physician assisted suicide are used to mean euthanasia, but these are not synonym with euthanasia.

Passive euthanasia is generally accepted worldwide. Active involuntary euthanasia is illegal in almost all countries. Practicing active voluntary euthanasia is illegal and considered as criminal homicide in most of the countries and will face punishment up to imprisonment for 14 years. While active involuntary euthanasia is legal in countries such as Netherland, Belgium, and Luxembourg; assisted suicide is legal in Switzerland and the united states of Oregon, Washington and Montana.

Manyactivists against euthanasia feel that legalizing euthanasia will lead to slippery slope phenomenon which leads to a greater number of non-voluntary euthanasia. It is proposed to formulate strict standard guidelines to practice euthanasia in countries where it is legalized, regulation of death and other practices like mandatory reporting of all cases of euthanasia, consulting with psychiatrist, obtaining second opinion, improved hospice care have to be followed for standardization of euthanasia.[19]

IX. THE THIRD I.E. THE FINAL FUNDAMENTAL ISSUES OF THE RESEARCH WORK—HOW DEATH SHOULD BE DIGNIFIED?

From the two important issues mentioned above related to this research work i.e. the terminal illness and the euthanasia, it is clear that these issues are closely related; because terminal illnesses certify the death of a person in near future, whereas, euthanasia provides a way how should a terminal ill personrecommend his own death within a stipulated time actively or passively. But there are other ways also through which the death of a terminal ill patient seems to be handled. Some of the ways pertaining to end-of-life care for the elderly are, hence, of great relevance. These are Palliative care, Life-prolonging treatment, Hospice care and telling the obvious.

Palliative care is the total active care of a patient whose disease is not responsive to any curative treatment. Palliative care, 'seeks to prevent, relieve or soothe the symptoms of disease or disorder without affecting a cure.' Here, the goal is to achieve the best possible quality of life for the patient and his/her family. It is the control of pain and other physical symptoms such as breathlessness, loss of appetite, insomnia, anxiety, depression, and so on. Relief from the symptoms may require administration of drugs or use of other procedures which are otherwise contraindicated. For example, the

EUTHANASIA: A COMPARATIVE STUDY BETWEEN WESTERN AND INDIAN VIEWS

administration of increasing dosages of sedatives and similar drugs for uncontrollable pain, breathlessness or insomnia may cause depression of respiration and other body functions yet, their medicines from the care of most of the palliative drug regimens. Palliative care is not designed to bring on an early death. It does not postpone death and prolong a miserable life. Palliative care is a multi-disciplinary approach and includes psychological, social and spiritual aspects of care.

Advance technology in modern times has introduced entirely new vistas in end-of-life care. The diseases, hitherto considered 'incurable', can well be partly controlled or cured. Similarly, lifespan can be prolonged or stretched and may be postponed. These advancements have enormously complicated the issues pertaining to end-of-life care more, so far, the elderly and especially, in resource limited countries like India. Furthermore, there are many social, religious, and spiritual and legal overtones involved here. Therapy concerning the transplantation of organs that have stopped functioning has challenged the concept of incurability. We can no more define a disease as incurable when organ replacement is available, in the case of progressive diseases like chronic renal, respiratory, cardiac and liver failure, leukaemia and other blood cancers. Sometimes, literally speaking, life is brought back from the jaws of death with the help of life prolonging treatments like assisted respiratory support, artificial maintenance of nutrition and hydration, cardiac pacing, and so on.

EUTHANASIA: A COMPARATIVE STUDY BETWEEN WESTERN AND INDIAN VIEWS

It is true that the life has been prolonged with the advantages of modern medical treatments. But there is question regarding the dignity of life, as well as the dignity of death. Whether life should be meaninglessly prolonged or ended at will is larger issue in medical, legal and in religious circles. This issue leads to a dilemma regarding the death of an individual as like as the dilemmas concerned with the individual's rights versus the rights, duties and resources of the family and so on.

When a terminal ill patient becomes sure about his/her death, he/she may take decision not to be hospitalized but to die in his/her own place. In a hospital, it is not possible to fulfil all the last desires of the patient. For this important reason most, elderly people would prefer to die at home, rather than in a hospital or nursing home. Hospice services, widely available in the western countries, offer medical services in a home like atmosphere. In the case of India, most elderly people die at home. An Indian family remains an ideal example of a well-knit social unit. Although, the compulsions of leading the fast life in accordance with earning more and more money is sometimes cased fragmentation and erosion of these traditional values. Therefore, it is logical to resort an organized, stable and dignified care of the elderly rather than leaving them isolated or unattended.

An important aspect of terminal care is also concerned with the art of disclosing the worst and of telling the truth, for instance, an incurable problem that may culminate in early death. In the case of the elderly, this is rather obvious; most of the aged patients expect death and wait for it to occur. Others may consider death as a merciful ending of disability, but everybody wants a peaceful and dignified death.

Indian Perspective of medical care at the end-of-life of an elderly individual, especially one who is sick, extends from the first encounter with the patient, to the period of bereavement. The Indian concept is that of inevitability and a graceful acceptance of the illness, old age and death. The terminal care should involve more of empathy than sympathy aimed at a dignified exit than a protracted existence and prolonged death. This results in a greater degree of satisfaction rather than frustration or guilt at the end.[20]

X. CONCLUSION CUM OBJECTIVE OF THE RESERCH WORK

From this backgroundit is clear, if euthanasia as well as the other ways of handling death for the terminal ill persons, isconsidered then what is true, from the Western perspective,these aretoo much mechanical, because the only purpose of hastening death is to give the relief the terminal ill patient from unbearable sufferings. 'For instance, the Dutch law on euthanasia refers to "unbearable suffering" as the criterion to request euthanasia. That is, this law refers on a subjective evaluation by the patient, not presenting any feasible alternatives to a death with dignity.'[21]Furthermore, there is a controversy, whether euthanasia as well as the other waysof

EUTHANASIA: A COMPARATIVE STUDY BETWEEN WESTERN AND INDIAN VIEWS

handling death isat all concerned with the feasible alternatives to a death with dignity or not.Everyone of this planet must have some values—instrumental and intrinsic. Even death should be dignified whether it is caused by the terminal illness or by normally. Euthanasia and the said other ways, being mechanical is failed to cover this point. If the Indian perspective is considered, though euthanasia has not been used in literal sense in Indian context, it may help the terminal ill patients to give a dignified death, because in Indian perspective each individual soul is immortal by nature [22] and continues to exist even after the death of the body. Indic view does not show much care about the body ailment. It emphasizes on the salvation of the individual soul. It does not totally follow the modern Western concept of euthanasia. In order to be emancipated or to keep the purity of soul, the Indians have permitted sati, *jauhar, saka, prayopavesa, santhara* etc. At the same time, it is needless to say;for a general human being, it is not possible to ignore the existence of body as a whole. That is why, neither Western euthanasia nor Indian euthanasia separately able to resolve this problem i.e. to find out a way through which the death should be dignified. A join ventured approach may be helpful in this regard. For this reason, in this thesis, a comparative study between Western and Indian euthanasia has been worked out in order to resolve this problem and choose the better way out for terminal ill patient.

EUTHANASIA: A COMPARATIVE STUDY BETWEEN WESTERN AND INDIAN VIEWS

Notes & References:

1. Abhedananda, Swami: *Life Beyond Death A Critical Study of Spiritualism*(4th Edition), Ramakrishna Vedanta Math, Kolkata, 1965, P-263

2. https://www.macmilandictionary.com

3. Nirvana, like the *UpanisadicĀtmā*, is repeated described by Buddha as calm (shānta), immortal (*amrta*), unproduced (*akrta*), uncaused (*asamskrta*), unborn (*ajata*), *undecaying*(*ajara*), undying (*amara*), eternal (*nitya*), abiding (*dhruva*), unchanging (*shashvata*), highest joy (*paramasukha*), blissful (Shiva), desire less (*tṛṣṇā-kṣaya*), cessation of plurality (*bhavarnirodha*; *prapanchopafhama*) and the fearless goal (*abhaya pada*). All the epithets (or their synonyms) which the *Upanisadic* seers use for the *Ātmā*, Buddha uses for Nirvana. *Ātmā* and *Nirvāna* stand for the Inexpressible and the Ineffable Absolute which is transcendent to thought and is realised through immediate spiritual experience (*bodhi* or *prajñā*). From Sharma, Chandradhar.: *The Advaita Tradition in Indian Philosophy A Study of Advaita in Buddhism, Vedānta and Kāshmira Shaivism,* Motilal Banarsidass Publishers Private Limited, Delhi, 2007, P-29

4. *Asabdamsparsamrupamavyayamtathaharasannityamagandhavaccayat/*

   Anadyanantammahatah param dhruvamnicayyatanmrtyumukhatpramucyate//—Katha Verse: 15. Chapter-3

5. Gupta, Mahendranath.: *Sri Sri Ramakrishna Kathamrita*,Volume 3, Udbodhon, Calcutta, 1902, P-174

6. *Hiranmayenapatrenasatyasyapihitammukham/*

   Tattvampusannapavrnusatyadharmayadrstyae//—Isha Verse 15)

7. *Pusannekarseyamasuryaprajapatyavyuharasminsamuha/*

   Tejahyatterupamkalyanatamamtattepasyamiyo'savasaupurusahso'hamasmi//—Isha Verse 16

8. *Vayuranilamamrtamathedambhasmantamsariram/*

   Om kratosmarakrtamsmara//—Isha Verse 17

9. *Agnenayasupatharayeasmanvisvani deva vayunanividvan/*

EUTHANASIA: A COMPARATIVE STUDY BETWEEN WESTERN AND INDIAN VIEWS

Yuyodhyasmajjuhuranamenobhuyisthamtenamauktimvidhema//Isha Verse—1

10. *Yathanadyahsyandamanahsamudre'stamgachhantinamarupevihaya/ Tathavidvannamarupadvimuktahparatparampurusamupaitidivyam//—Mandukya* Verse—3.2.8

11. *Andhyamtamahpravisantiye'sambhutimupasate/ Tato bhuyaivatetamoya u sambhutyamratah//Isha* Verse—12

12. *Vāsāṁsijīrṇāniyathāvihāyanavānigṛhṇātinaro'parāṇi | Tathāśarīrāṇivihāyajīrṇāny-anyānisaṁyātinavānidehī ||* Chapter-2, Verse-22 of the *Gitā*

13. *Śarīraṃyadavāpnotiyaccāpy-utkrāmat-īśvaraḥ/ Gṛhītvaitānisaṃyātivāyur-gandhānivāśayāt// Śrotraṃcakṣuḥsparśanaṃ ca rasanaṃghrāṇameva ca/ Adhiṣṭhāyamanaścāyaṃ viṣayānupasevate// Utkrāmantaṃsthitaṃ vāpibhuñjānaṃ vāguṇān-vitam/ Vimūḍhānānupaśyantipaśyantijñāna-cakṣuṣaḥ// Yatantoyoginaścainaṃpaśyanty-ātmany-avasthitam/ Yatanto'pyakṛtātmānonainaṃpaśyantyacetasaḥ//* Chapter-15, Verse-08-11 of the *Gitā*

14. Chatterjee, ChoraSuhita., Patnaik, Priyadarshi., Chariar, Vijayraghaban.M. (Ed.): *Discourses on Aging and Dying*, SAGE publications India Pvt. Ltd, 2008

15. [Https:// Plato.stanford.edu, *The definition of death (Stanford encyclopedia of philosophy)*

16. Ibid.

17. Ibid.

18. Hudson, P., Hudson R., Philip, J.:*Legalizing physician assisted suicide and/or euthanasia: Pragmatic implication. Palliative Care and Supportive Care*, Cambridge University Press, 2015

EUTHANASIA: A COMPARATIVE STUDY BETWEEN WESTERN AND INDIAN VIEWS

19. Bada Math, Suresh.,Chaturvedi, Santosh. K.: *Euthanasia: Right to life Vs right to die*, in *Indian Journal of Medicine & Research*, Vol. 136(6), December 2012, pp. 899-902

20. Jindal, S.K.: *Old Age, Disease and Terminal Care: A Hindu Perspective* in Chatterjee, ChoraSuhita., Patnaik, Priyadarshi., Chariar, Vijayraghaban, M. (Ed.): *Discourses on Aging and Dying*, SAGE publications India Pvt. Ltd, 2008, pp. 217-224

21. Nunes, Rui., Rego, Guilhermina.: *Euthanasia: A Challenge to Medical Ethics*, in Journal *of Clinical Research and Bioethics*, Volume 16, Issue 4, 2016, P-2

22. Chatterjee, Chora Suhita., Patnaik, Priyadarshi., Chariar, Vijayraghaban, M. (Ed.): *Discourses on Aging and Dying, Introductory Chapter*, SAGE publications India Pvt. Ltd, 2008, pp.15-29

> There is little to be found in medical writings on the management of the dying, or on the treatment best adapted to the relief of the sufferings incident to that condition. The subject is not specially taught in any of ourmedical schools; and the young physicianentering on the active duties of his officehas to learn for himself, as best he may,what to do, and what not to do, in the most solemn and delicate position in whichhe can be placed,in attendance on thedying, and administering the resources ofthe medical art, in aid of an easy, gentle,and placid death.— Munk William: *Euthanasia*, Longmans Green& Co., New York, 1887, P-4

CHAPTER: 2

Euthanasia & It's Types

EUTHANASIA: A COMPARATIVE STUDY BETWEEN WESTERN AND INDIAN VIEWS

CHAPTER: 2

Euthanasia & It's Types

I will give no deadly medicine to any one if asked, nor suggest any counsel.
—*The Hippocratic Oath.*

I. INTRODUCTION

From the introductory chapter, it is clear that the chief aims of this research work are to make a comparative study between the Western concept of euthanasia and the Indian concept of euthanasia in order to find out a way through which the death of a person, especially terminal ill patient could be dignified. The death should be dignified, because human being has an intrinsic value. He has the right to live with dignity. He wants to continue his or her activity throughout the life in some form or other, because the activities and only activities make a human life meaningful. If the life becomes inactive, there is no meaning of living. In a broad sense, however, from the perspective of Big Bang theory, as the universe is still in the process of creation, each and every entity of this universe whether it is animate or inanimate are active. But this type of activity, though universal, does not related to the meaningfulness of human life. In case of incurable diseases, when human being comes to know that, his or her normal activities of life seem to be a quick end, naturally, his or her meaningful life also comes to an end very shortly. That is why

EUTHANASIA: A COMPARATIVE STUDY BETWEEN WESTERN AND INDIAN VIEWS

he or she may demand that his or her life must be come to an end with dignity. One may ask: what will happen in case of the aged persons. The aged persons are not at all, as like as the terminal ill patients, as terminal ill patients are informed by the doctors suddenly about their inability of the treatment following the current medical science which could cure them. Side by side, the aged persons, after leading their meaningful life, could easily spend their life in home with their future generations.

However, Euthanasia is closely related to end the life of a terminal ill patient i.e. to hastening the death of a terminal ill patient in order to relief him or her from the unbearable sufferings. Whether euthanasia can be the best way to dignify the death or not, is not the focal point of this chapter, rather this chapter attempts to make a thorough study on euthanasia which covers the definition of euthanasia, the relation between sufferings and euthanasia, merciful killing and euthanasia, types of euthanasia and their justifications, debates on the moral preference of active and different types of euthanasia like customs in India such as *Santhara*, *Sati* or *Jauhar*, *Prayopavesa*, and *Mahasamadhi*.

II. EUTHANASIA, WHAT IT IS?

Though the term 'euthanasia' has been used by Francis Bacon in a medical context in 17th century, in order to refer to an easy, painless, happy death when the patient has been in a critical condition; the first apparent usage of the term 'euthanasia' belonged to the historian Suetonius, who used the

EUTHANASIA: A COMPARATIVE STUDY BETWEEN WESTERN AND INDIAN VIEWS

term to convey how the Emperor Augustus had died quickly, without being suffered for a long time, in the arms of his wife, *Livia*. According to Bacon, it was the sole responsibility of a physician to ease the 'physical sufferings' of the body of a patient. Being one of the great profounder of Inductive Logic, Bacon applied the expression 'outward euthanasia' in order to exclude any kind of spiritual linkage concerned with euthanasia. Following Bacon, at present the term euthanasia has been defined as the 'painless inducement of a quick death.' However, from the etymological perspective, the term euthanasia is derived from Greek, EU meaning good and *Thanatos* meaning death. Put together, it means good death. Naturally, euthanasia may be defined as the hastening of death of a patient to prevent further sufferings.

It may be argued that the approaches made above in order to understand the concept of euthanasia, have been failed to give a unanimous cum universal understanding regarding the meaning of the concept of euthanasia, as it leaves open a number of possible controversies. Because there are possibilities of getting to be killed painlessly by other process such as through an accident, but these will not be treated as euthanasia. For this reason, the concept of euthanasia should be examined in such a way that there would not be any possible controversies. In fact, the concept of euthanasia is linked with some other essential factors also and those factors should be explored. Amongst these essential factors, suffering is one. That is why the Oxford Dictionary incorporates suffering as a necessary condition and defines euthanasia as 'the painless killing of a patient suffering from an incurable and painful disease or in an irreversible coma.' It is noteworthy to mention here, this definition adds two extra factors: one is the patient has been suffering from the incurable disease for a long time and the other is the patient may be in a coma for a lengthy period.

From this, it is clear that the concept of euthanasia is not just a simple concept, because it is attached to the killing of human being rather than any other animal. That is why the intention of killing should be crystal clear. Naturally, the other important point which is concerned with euthanasia is the intention of killing. Some definitions of euthanasia, for this reason, incorporate that the death must be intended, rather than being accidental, and the intention of the action must be a 'merciful death'. For this reason, perhaps, Peter singer in his book 'Practical Ethics' accepts the lexicographical meaning of euthanasia as 'a mild and easy death' and adds that now it signifies the killing of those persons who are sick and aged for saving them from further misery or crisis. In addition to this he says that euthanasia is defined as the hastening of death of a patient to prevent further suffering [1]

III. DIFFERENT TYPES OF EUTHANASIA

From the above, it is clear, euthanasia is no doubt, is linked with the killing of a person who has been suffering from incurable pain and whose life has been turned as a burden to

EUTHANASIA: A COMPARATIVE STUDY BETWEEN WESTERN AND INDIAN VIEWS

him-self as well as to others. In order to get relief from that particular condition, euthanasia may be applied following the consent of the person who is the subject to consider euthanasia. It should be mentioned here that euthanasia is not murder or suicide, though euthanasia could never be understood without having the concept of killing. It is not murder, as the intention of the person who assists for euthanasia is clear—to give relief from unbearable pain of the terminal ill patient.

Again, it is not suicide, because the decision of suicide is taken by only that person who commits suicide, whereas in case of euthanasia, the terminal ill patent is not the only person who can take the decision of ending his own life. So, it is clear that euthanasia is different from either murder or suicide, but the notion of killing can never be ignored. That is why the notion of provoking for injustice may act as the shadow of euthanasia. However, euthanasia may be conducted with or the without the consent of the patient. On the basis of giving the consent of the patient, in general, there are three types of Euthanasia—1] Voluntary Euthanasia—where the patient is in a position to give his consent, 2] In-voluntary Euthanasia—where the patient does not give his consent, and 3] Non-voluntary Euthanasia—where the patient is not in a position either to give the consent or to deny to give the consent. Peter Singer remarks in his book 'Practical Ethics' that these three types of euthanasia may raise different ethical issues. Following Peter Singer, let us consider about the justifiability of each type of euthanasia after the discussion of these threefold Euthanasia.

EUTHANASIA: A COMPARATIVE STUDY BETWEEN WESTERN AND INDIAN VIEWS

III.I VOLUNTARY EUTHANASIA

The expression Voluntary Euthanasia indicates that type of Euthanasia which is depended on the willingness of the concerned persons who are somehow associated with the Euthanasia directly or indirectly. In order to clarify Voluntary Euthanasia, Peter singer says in his book, 'Practical Ethics' that the decision of Voluntary Euthanasia is entertained only when the patient has been suffering from an incurable disease with extreme pain and he is in a position to give consent about his hastening death along with his nearest family members. Here, the dignity of autonomy is revered and there is no scope through which anyone can say that the choice is irrational. In fact, if there is no scope for survival following the knowledge of upgraded medical science, it is better to honour the will of the concerned patient. [2]

In case of Voluntary Euthanasia, the willingness of two types of persons is involved—i) persons who are able to express their willingness and (ii) the persons who are unable to do so. Among these two types, the first one is not problematical, but those who are unable to express their will due to coma may be problematic. One may say that it should be taken at par with the non voluntary euthanasia, because the patient is not in a position to give his or her consent. But it should be noted here that in coma, none can give his or her consent, but it is possible for any healthy person to give his consent about euthanasia prior to an accident which leads him or her to the state of coma.

EUTHANASIA: A COMPARATIVE STUDY BETWEEN WESTERN AND INDIAN VIEWS

Any healthy person should prepare a draft of written request for euthanasia. It may be a controversial issue to settle a firm decision about one's own death, because any one whoever he or she may be, loves his or own life. So, there must be a provision of the re-affirmation of the decision taken by him or her about Euthanasia time to time. If a person is known as incapable of making or expressing a decision to die, because of his or her mental inability, though he or she has been in intolerable pain, other nearest person of that concerned person can act as a proxy for that particular patient. In that case, however, Peter Singer remarked, it will be very hard to make a water tight compartmental distinction between euthanasia and assisted suicide.

However, the Voluntary Euthanasia may be further classified as non-aggressive and aggressive. In case of non-aggressive voluntary euthanasia, the common treatments which are applied by the medical practitioners such as antibiotics or analgesics or surgery or the use of life saving drugs or the administration of strong medications where morphine is used to relieve pain are withheld. As a result, non-aggressive Euthanasia sometimes may be controversial. Terri *Schiavo*, a Floridian had been in a vegetative state since 1990, for example, has died when her feeding tube has been removed in 2005 by her husband. Her husband as well as the then government had to face some agitation and social controversy at that time. Her husband claimed that her wife would have considered doing

EUTHANASIA: A COMPARATIVE STUDY BETWEEN WESTERN AND INDIAN VIEWS

this, but it was too difficult to be confirmed as she had no living will and the rest of her family claimed otherwise.

Aggressive euthanasia, on the other hand, entails the direct use of lethal substances or forces to kill by the doctors, it is in fact, most controversial. Historical evidences show at the time of World War II, the Nazis in Germany, carried out an involuntary euthanasia programme in secret where a lots of children were killed as they were treated as unfit—'a life unworthy to be lived' due to mental retardation or physical deformity or other debilitating problems. It was a hidden and confirmed belief of Nazis' eugenics programme that they could never raise a superior Aryan race unless they could not kill the children who were born with physical and mental challenged.

In fact, Euthanasia in the form of aggressive and non-aggressive, have been marked as active and passive euthanasia. There is an interesting debate regarding the moral ground of preference of these two types of Euthanasia as pointed out and discussed by James *Rachels* which has been analyzed later on in this chapter.

In order to explain the point that there is no water tight compartmental distinction between euthanasia and assisted suicide, Peter singer shows three different examples of Voluntary Euthanasia performed by Jean *Humphry*, Janet Adkins and George *Zygmaniak*. Jean *Humphry* was a cancer patient and asked her husband Derek *Humphry* to hasten her death so that she could over come from the unbearable pain. In

EUTHANASIA: A COMPARATIVE STUDY BETWEEN WESTERN AND INDIAN VIEWS

response to her wife's willing, Derek gave some tablets to Jean and she died after swallowing the tablets. Now, the point is: Jean was supported by her husband in order to die quickly, in other words her husband assisted Jean to die by giving the tablets as soon as possible. So, here it is very difficult indeed to make the distinction between voluntary euthanasia and assisted suicide.

The Voluntary Euthanasia went one step further, as Peter Singer pointed out, when a Michigan pathologist Dr. Jac Kevorkian built a suicide machine. It helped to commit suicide for those who were permanently ill. This machine was equipped with three separate bottles containing a metal and a pole with the attachments of tubes to the bottles. The intravenous drips were supplied through this tube. The doctor used to insert the tube into the patient's vein. A special solution with saline entered into the body. The patient can then press a switch through which the coma-induced drug passed from the tube to the body. And finally, the third bottle started to follow automatically which was full of a deadly drug in order to kill the patient. The doctor announced that he wanted to use the machine for a permanently ill patient as the Michigan law permit it.

In June 1990, Janet Adkins was diagnosed with Alzheimer's disease and he decided to end his life. He made a contact with Dr. Kevorkian and informed about his wishes. He wished death, rather than go through the slow and progressive degradation

EUTHANASIA: A COMPARATIVE STUDY BETWEEN WESTERN AND INDIAN VIEWS

associated with the disease. Dr. Kevorkian not only helped Janet Adkins to die but also assisted him how to use the machine. Not only that, he also informed the police that Janet Adkins was died by using his newly invented machine. Though Dr. Kevorkian was initially charged with the case of murder, it was the verdict of the Judge that Janet Adkins was the cause of his own death and he did not allow the allegation taken by the police. The following year Dr. Kevorkian used his device again in order to hasten the death of two terminal ill patients.

Peter Singer then cited some examples of people who were willing to die but unable to kill themselves. In the year 1973, George Zygmaniak was admitted to the hospital after being injured in a motor accident near by his home in New-Jersey. His whole body became paralyzed from his neck and he was in extreme pain. He told his doctor and his brother Lester that he did not want to survive in this condition. George begged them both to kill him. Lester asked the doctors and hospital staff about his recovery, but they could not answer. Lester then took a gun to the hospital and asked the permission of his brother. George made a positive response by nodding his head. Lester then shot his brother. Peter Singer remarked the incident made by George was a clear example of Voluntary Euthanasia, although some safe guards should be taken to legalize Voluntary Euthanasia.

Let it be noted, Peter singer claims in this regard that the case of *Zygmaniak*, is no doubt a case of clear instance of

EUTHANASIA: A COMPARATIVE STUDY BETWEEN WESTERN AND INDIAN VIEWS

Voluntary Euthanasia because—(a) George *Zygmaniak's* desire of death was of a fixed and rational kind, (b) this instances based on the best available information about his situation, (c) George *Zygmaniak's* killing was not carried out by a doctor and (d) in this instance, there are no bar of medical opinions.

III.II JUSTIFICATION OF VOLUNTARY EUTHANASIA

Though the concept of euthanasia is loaded with moral debates, as there is always a chance of misuse of taking life in the name of euthanasia for the sake of extra economical advantages, we may imagine an ideal discourse where all the conditions of euthanasia has been fulfilled. In that case, from the perspective of morality, euthanasia may be acceptable for the sake of easy and gentle death of terminal ill patients. But, it has not been taken as a public health policy by all the countries. Some morally acceptable principles may not be supported by the law. Again, some principles which are not morally justified can be supported by the law. For this reason, the justification of euthanasia should be taken into consideration. It may be the case that in future, the euthanasia will become as normal as like as an operation. However, at present, in case of euthanasia, it is clear that unbearable sick patients have been in turmoil due to the prevailing laws in most countries. When these patients are asking the doctors to end their lives so that they can get rid of the unbearable pain, there is a risk which is faced by the doctors to be charged the case of homicide. Proponents of Voluntary Euthanasia suggest that the

EUTHANASIA: A COMPARATIVE STUDY BETWEEN WESTERN AND INDIAN VIEWS

law should be changed in such a way that a doctor can be authorised to prescribe what is intended by the terminal ill patients. In 1980, the courts of Netherlands reviewed various decisions and made certain conditions. After meeting these conditions, the doctors in the Netherlands are empowered to prescribe openly Voluntary Euthanasia. In Germany, the doctors can provide his patient a way to end his life, but cannot deliver the material to the patient which may be the cause of death. Death may be a useful friend for those who have been seeking Voluntary Euthanasia. If we critically review this type of euthanasia, we can say that only rationalists, self-conscious and self-determined persons are eligible to give consent about their own death, though at the time it may be true, at the verge of their own death they may not be rational and conscious, because of the illness. Peter singer comments that we need to review how policy matters differ when a person raises question about his own decision about Voluntary Euthanasia. He makes some criteria in this regard.

    a) The first is related to the utilitarianism. They claim that since self-conscious people are capable of fearing their own death, killing them-selves has a worse effect on others.

    b) The second is the most important reason against killing according to the priority calculation is to count the desire to survive as failure.

    c) The third is related to the theory of rights where a person can have the right to life and any desire

EUTHANASIA: A COMPARATIVE STUDY BETWEEN WESTERN AND INDIAN VIEWS

whatever it may be should be tied up with the existence.

d) The fourth is related to the respect for the autonomous decision of the agents.

Now, we can apply the above mentioned criteria when a person will to die as he has been suffering from a painful and incurable disease. The objection of utilitarianism cannot be applied to those who assist suicide after getting the consent of the victims. When such people die in this situation, there will be no tendency of generating of fear or insecurity, since this assisted suicide is occurred only when the unconditional consent is given. In fact, if no initiative is taken to follow the Voluntary Euthanasia after the fulfilment of all the conditions, there is a chance of the spread of fear due to the unnecessarily delayed of death and prolonging the suffering. In a case study based on the government of the Netherlands, it has been found that many patients asked their doctors to help them in such way that they could avoid prolonged unbearable pain. Preference utilitarianism, however, are not against Voluntary Euthanasia.

According to the theory of rights, Voluntary Euthanasia is also an essential feature of rights. If anyone is given the right to life, following the theory of right to life, he or she should be given the right to freedom of his own life including the will not to be alive. Singer says when any one allows giving the right to make entry into his private life and in that case, if nothing is

EUTHANASIA: A COMPARATIVE STUDY BETWEEN WESTERN AND INDIAN VIEWS

taken as absurd; then when a person allows the doctors to take the right of his or her life, it will be treated as usual. This is because his right to privacy has not been violated since his right has been left to his neighbours by himself. Similarly, his right to life will not be violated if the doctor ends his life at his or her request.

The principle of respect for autonomy allows the agents to lead a life free from repression or interference. When a rational agent chooses to die freely, then it is our duty to respect the autonomy. Some opponents of the legalization of Voluntary Euthanasia may say that death can never be the subject which can be taken independently as well as logically. None can say that the sick are not be pressurized by their relatives to end their lives quickly. This point is not actually a strong argument against euthanasia, but a technical issue is related to euthanasia. The following guideline may be followed made by the court.

- It is administered by the registered senior doctors only.
- The patient's decision should be based on his strong mental health condition.
- The patient has an incredible condition that results in prolonged physical or mental pain that the patient finds unbearable.
- There is rational approach from the patient's point of view to reduce the patient's suffering.

EUTHANASIA: A COMPARATIVE STUDY BETWEEN WESTERN AND INDIAN VIEWS

- The doctor also consulted with an independent professional who agrees with his or her opinion.

Following all these guidelines, the Royal Dutch Medical Association and the common people in the Netherlands strongly support euthanasia and still now any dispute is yet to be noticed regarding euthanasia in the Netherlands.

In the euthanasia debate, it is often said that the doctors may be the victim of taking a wrong decision. Peter Singer holds that this cannot be taken as the sufficient condition to ban euthanasia. What will be the alternative to reduce the pain? When all the ways of medical science have been proved as impotent, euthanasia is applied. Elisabeth Kubler-Ross, however, has claimed in his book, *'Death and Dying'* that none of her patients request euthanasia for the execution, though at the initial level, they have asked for euthanasia. She said that in her Palliative Care, the patient gradually used to learn how to accept their deaths with and without having pain. Peter singer thinks *Kubler* Ross may be right. This may relieve nausea or other annoying side effects, but unfortunately a minority of patients who die now, have this kind of care. Peter singer says, it will probably be possible in one day to treat all the temporarily ill and incurable patients in this way and no one will request euthanasia anymore and the matter will become a non-issue. But it is now just a utopian norm. Euthanasia cannot be denied to those who have to die and to survive in the least comfortable conditions.

EUTHANASIA: A COMPARATIVE STUDY BETWEEN WESTERN AND INDIAN VIEWS

III.III NON-VOLUNTARY EUTHANASIA

In case of non-voluntary euthanasia, Peter Singer points out that the patient is not in a position to make the distinction between what is life and what is death. In fact, the patient is in coma or in vegetative state. [3] If a patient is not able to understand the choice between life and death, then euthanasia will not be voluntary or involuntary but non-voluntary. This situation can include people who are sick, seriously disabled children who unable to consent, aging people who are unable to understand what euthanasia is, and the persons who previously requested for euthanasia but later on refused euthanasia. Peter Singer remarks several cases of non-voluntary euthanasia have been settled in the court and also become the subject of popular news. Amongst these popular cases, the case of killing of a child by his father may be note worthy. Louis *Repouille* had a blind child who had been bedridden since childhood. According to the *Repouille*, he was always lying like a dead man. He could neither walk nor speak. In fact, he could not do anything. Eventually, *Repouille* killed his son with chloroform. Here, the child was not in a position to give the consent about his or her death, because he or she did not understand what the meaning of life was.

Peter Singer then shows an incident of 1988 where it has been observed, sometimes, modern medical facility may force people to apply non-voluntary euthanasia. A child named Samuel Linares swallowed a small object and stuck it in the air pipe. As a result, oxygen could not reach in the brain. The child went into a coma. The baby was admitted to a Chicago hospital in coma condition. The baby was placed on a breathing apparatus. After the passing of eight months when the healthy condition of the baby remained the same, the hospital planned to transfer the child to a long-term care unit. Shortly before this step, Samuel's parents went to see their baby. When the Child's mother left the hospital, the child's father pulled out a gun and told the nurse to stay away. The child was then disconnected its respiratory tract by his or her father until the children died. Convinced of Samuel's death, he dropped his gun and surrendered to police. He was charged by murder. But the grand jury, however, refused to prove the murder charge and was given a lenient sentence on a minor charge raised as a result of the use of the gun. Obviously, such events are different from voluntary euthanasia. The importance of these events lies in the fact whether these types of incidents are happened for the sake of families or not. *Repouille* killed his son as he could no longer bear the pain of the child. The same mental condition may be assumed for Samuel Linares when he killed his son.

III.IV JUSTIFICATION OF NON-VOLUNTARY EUTHANASIA

It has been observed that non-voluntary euthanasia is applied only when the patient is not in a position to give consent for his own death. Acute intellectual disabled child from the birth and coma patients are the examples who are supposed to be the members of the set of non-voluntary euthanasia persons. The opposition may argue that it is not legitimate to go for non-

EUTHANASIA: A COMPARATIVE STUDY BETWEEN WESTERN AND INDIAN VIEWS

voluntary euthanasia as the patient is not in a position to give his or her consent. We have an obligation to protect the life. We should left the life of the patient to the will of the God.

But Peter Singer says that being human species we have a social life. Belonging of two legs and two arms are not the real mark of human beings. Human beings must be intelligent. Those who have been in a vegetative condition for a long time are nothing but the burden to the family as well as the society. Society does not value the inactive, unconscious and vegetative human beings. That is why if these types of persons are categorised under the set of supposed to be non-voluntary euthanasia person then none would be charged in murder case, because killing them cannot be equivalent to killing the ordinary people or any other self-conscious persons. The birth of a child is usually a joy for parents and a natural bonding is observed between the parents and the child. Due to the effect of this bonding, some parents give the consent for euthanasia. But some other parents may deny giving their consent for euthanasia; rather they would say that let the disable child live as long as possible. In fact, no parents want to kill their child in the name of non- voluntary euthanasia. When the parent realise that their child is not at all normal but born with several disabilities, the medical facilities are limited and it is impossible to bear the cost of hospital, the parents may go for non voluntary euthanasia.

EUTHANASIA: A COMPARATIVE STUDY BETWEEN WESTERN AND INDIAN VIEWS

Being a follower of the utilitarianism as propounded by the nineteenth century philosopher Jeremy Bentham and developed by J.S. Mill, Peter Singer applies the greatest happiness to the greatest numbers—the basic principle of utilitarianism to justify the different kinds of euthanasia. The utilitarianism judges an action on the basis of its consequences where the chief purpose of any action is to shorten the pain and increase the happiness. Peter Singer, however, gives importance on the equality of the interests which seems to be the refined version of the utilitarianism of Mill. It may be called as preference utilitarianism. Here the actions are not judged by the consequences i.e. decreasing the pain and the increasing of the happiness. But the ways through which the concerned persons are to perform the actions. If all of my friends, for example, in my birthday party, announce they will not eat the cake due to the control of diet; then I can get the large portion of the cake. Similarly, those babies who have been suffering from different kinds of incurable diseases, following the preference utilitarianism, the parents can decide to go for non-voluntary euthanasia. Peter Singer's argument can be criticized in the ground that any new born baby is subject to be killed by the decision taken by the parents on the basis of the skin, hair, colour, or sex or the length of their legs of the new born babies instead of they have not been suffering from any kind of incurable diseases. But none is the above of law. A strong medical guide line should be followed by the parents as well as the doctors before taking such decision. Neonates should be allowed to die if and only if they are actually suffering from truly incurable diseases such as *Spina* bifida or *Down's Syndrome*.

III.V INVOLUNTARY EUTHANASIA

In case of Involuntary Euthanasia, the concerned person is neither in a position to give his consent nor does he give his positive response when he is asked for euthanasia, though he has been in a tremendous unbearable pain or not in a position to feel the pain. From the perspective of the agony of the concerned patient, the family members may favour for euthanasia, though the patient does not favour it. In fact, Involuntary Euthanasia is executed only when the concerned person is incapable of making any decision about his death or there is a chance of rejecting of the execution of euthanasia by the concerned person, due to the strong conviction on the God and is thus left to a proxy. [4] The word proxy is very much significant as well as highly controversial from the perspective of legality and morality of euthanasia for any self-conscious human being whoever he may be.

III.VI JUSTIFICATION OF INVOLUNTARY EUTHANASIA

In case of Voluntary Euthanasia, it is justifiable where the genuine consent has been received. But in case of involuntary euthanasia, there is no chance of receiving any consent and there may be a chance of going against euthanasia. Now, the question is: would it ever be possible to justify involuntary euthanasia on the ground to save one from extreme agony?

EUTHANASIA: A COMPARATIVE STUDY BETWEEN WESTERN AND INDIAN VIEWS

A human, being self-conscious favours euthanasia, only when he feels that his life is so bad due to the routine illness, it is not worth living anymore. When other person gives a proxy for the euthanasia, he actually applies the argument of analogy like this:

Anyone who has been suffering from genuine routine illness, consent for euthanasia, as he feels that it is not worth living anymore.

The person x has been suffering from genuine routine illness and it can be assumed that he feels it is not worth living anymore.

Therefore, the person x should give his consent for euthanasia.

This analogical argument depends on a presupposition that value of life should be equal to everyone. But, this is not possible, because the parameters of the value of life are not same to all. That is why Peter Singer remarks, 'It is not clear that we are ever justified to having much confidence in our judgments about whether the life of another person is, to that person, worth living.'[5] One may argue for Involuntary Euthanasia, on the ground that it may be permitted only when the concerned person is not in a position to feel his agony for future.

But in that case, the possibility of killing innocent children cannot be stopped. History shows, at the time of World War II, a lots of disabled children were killed when the Nazis in Germany, carried out an Involuntary Euthanasia programme, in secret, on the principle—'a life unworthy to be lived' to form a superior Aryan race. For this reason, Peter Singer says,

> If in real life we are unlikely ever to encounter a case of justifiable involuntary euthanasia, then it may be best to dismiss from our minds the fanciful; cases in which one might imagine defending it, and treat the rules against involuntary euthanasia as, for all practical purpose, absolute. [6]

III. RACHELS ON ACTIVE OR PASSIVE EUTHANASIA

When euthanasia is categorised as active or passive, on the basis of the nature of the involvement of those who are directly or indirectly engage to hasten the life of the terminal ill patent to give them relief from their unbearable pain, it has been noticed that Active Euthanasia, from the perspective of morality, is treated worse than the Passive Euthanasia. 'The important difference between active and passive euthanasia is that, in passive euthanasia, the doctor does not do anything to bring about the patient' death. The doctor does nothing, and the patient dies of whatever ills already afflict him. In active euthanasia, however, the doctor does something to bring about the patient's death: he kills him. The doctor who gives the patient with cancer a lethal injection has himself caused his patient's death; whereas if he merely ceases treatment, the cancer is the cause of the death.' [7] But Rachels argues there is no logical ground through which it can be concluded that Passive Euthanasia is morally better than the Active

EUTHANASIA: A COMPARATIVE STUDY BETWEEN WESTERN AND INDIAN VIEWS

Euthanasia, rather both of these should be deserved the same status.

In order to prove this claim, Rachels puts forward two fold arguments amongst which the first fold arguments are based on effective evidences where he closely analyses some case studies on terminal ill patients. Whereas the second fold arguments are based on reasoning where he shows that there is no significant moral ground through which active and passive euthanasia could be differentiate though it is, in general, accepted by the doctors that killing a terminal ill person directly is morally worse than letting die.

III.I.I ARGUMENT—I FROM EFFECTIVE EVIDENCE

Let us start with the first fold of argument where he talks about a patient who has been suffering from throat cancer. He will die in a few days, if the current medical system is not interrupted. But the patient and his family members ask the doctor to end the life as quick as possible in order to give relief from unbearable pain. Rachels says, let us assume, according to conventional doctrine, that the doctors stop the treatment. The decision of withholding treatment does not help the patient to die within a short period what the patient and his family ask for, but to suffer from the unbearable pain. If the relief from pain is the main focus of the patient, and his or her family, then withholding treatment is failed to give any expected result. So, it is illegitimate to prolong the suffering of the patient unnecessarily by stopping the treatment. On the other hand, if a

EUTHANASIA: A COMPARATIVE STUDY BETWEEN WESTERN AND INDIAN VIEWS

lethal injection is applied directly, the main purpose that is to give the relief from pain will be served. This fact provides reason to think that Active Euthanasia, once initiated not to prolong the suffering of the patient, becomes a reality, instead of the Passive Euthanasia is preferred. In other words, to support Passive Euthanasia instead of Active Euthanasia leads to more suffering than less. To quote Rachels,

> This fact provides strong reason for thinking that, once the initial decision not to prolong his agony has been made active euthanasia is actually preferable to passive euthanasia, rather than the reverse. [8]

Rachels points out that the process of allowing let dying can be relatively slow and painful for the patient. Whereas, using of the lethal injection is seemed to be better. He cites another example of the children who are born with 'Down's Syndrome'. In the United States, 01 (one) of 600 (six hundred) babies is born with 'Down's Syndrome'. These children have intestinal defects and need surgery for their survival. In these cases, the parents and the doctor decide not to operate and let the baby die following the Passive Euthanasia. When the operation is rejected, the doctors allow the children to die following the natural biological process. The body naturally fights against collapsing and tries as far as possible to delay the death. But from the perspective of a medical person, it is no doubt a tiring experience to observe a small child who is dying due to the infection and dehydration. Rachels argues that there are some people who may go against any type of euthanasia, but such children should not be allowed to die after suffering from hourly infection and dehydration which is clearly brutal.

III.I.II ARGUMENT—II FROM EFFECTIVE EVIDENCE

Rachels' second argument is that conventional doctrine decides life and death on irrelevant grounds. The life and the death of a baby cannot be decided on the basis of a particular deformity. If the intention is to save the life of a child, the operation must be arranged by the surgeon when a child is suffering from obstruction in intestinal tract. If the intention is not to save the life of a child, the operation may be withheld. As the child has been born with 'Down's Syndrome', let him or her die, can never be the ground of deciding factor of life and death, because there are many cases where these types of children survive without any operation, dies even if there is no such operation is arranged and survive after operation. He argues if a simple operation is required, it should not be stopped. If one thinks that this kind of child should not survive, it makes no difference that it is due to a blocked bowel tract. Thus he remarks,

> If the life of such an infant is worth preserving, what does it matter if it needs a simple operation? Or, if one thinks it better that such a baby should not live on, what difference does it make that it happens to have an unobstructed intestinal tract? In either case, the matter of life and death is being decided on irrelevant grounds. It is the Down's syndrome, and not the intestines, that is the issue. [9]

III.I.III ARGUMENT—I FROM REASONING

Rachels thinks that there is no significant moral ground through which active and passive euthanasia could be

EUTHANASIA: A COMPARATIVE STUDY BETWEEN WESTERN AND INDIAN VIEWS

differentiate though it is in general accepted by the doctors that killing a terminal ill person is morally worse than letting die. Rachels makes an extensive analysis by citing two situations where in situation—1 a person is killed by other person for the sake of huge property and in situation—2 a person is not killed directly but the circumstances compels the person to die for the sake of huge property by the other person.

In order to elaborate the first situation, we may take the example of a person Smith who had a 6 year old cousin. Smith's legacy would be benefited neatly, if something happens to his cousin. One day while his cousin was taking bath, Smith got a chance to fulfil his long lasted secret interest and at once drowned his cousin and then arranged the whole things in such a way that it would have been looked like an accident.

The second case is almost same with the first, but here Jones also planned to kill his 6-years old cousin for the sake of property. One day Jones saw that his cousin slip in the bathroom after getting hit in his head accidently and his face got drowned. Jones was standing next to his cousin and he was supposed to hold his head in the water. However, there was no need to press the head. After scattering a bit, the child drowned himself, as he saw that Jones did not do anything and die.

In case of situation number—1, Smith killed the child. But in case situation number—2, Jones allowed the child to die. The motives of these two incidents were the same i.e. to be the owner of the huge property. The only difference between these two, from the perspective of moral ground, is that Jones can claim his behaviour is less reprehensible than Smith's behaviour. But the question is: Is the difference between killing and letting die is itself a matter of moral importance. From the legal point of view, Jones may argue in court to save him-self that he just stood there and saw the cousin drowning, he didn't kill him as like as Jones. But from the moral perspective, if a person knows how to swim and allow someone to be drowned in water in front of him, seems to be worse than killing the person. That is why Rachels remarks,

> Moreover, suppose Jones pleaded, in his own defense, "After all, I didn't do anything except just stand there and watch the child drown. I didn't kill him; I only let him die." Again, if letting die were in itself less bad than killing, this defense should have at least some weight. But it does not. Such a 'defense' can only be regarded as a grotesque perversion of moral reasoning. Morally speaking, it is no defense at all. [10]

But in case of doctors, there is no question of personal gain. Euthanasia is allowed only in cases where the patient's life has a terrible burden for him-self and his family. Here the doctors argue that they will do nothing directly in order to end the life of the concerned patient that is why their performance is better than direct killing. Rachels counters the doctor's argument by saying that from the perspective of humanitarian ground the doctors deny to take life of other human beings directly and prefer let them die. But on the same humanitarian ground,

EUTHANASIA: A COMPARATIVE STUDY BETWEEN WESTERN AND INDIAN VIEWS

Rachels adds, the doctors should give the relief from unbearable pain who have been suffering from incurable diseases.

III.II.I ARGUMENT—II FROM REASONING

Now the point is, why active euthanasia where direct killing is involved; is treated as worse than letting die. In other words, why letting die is comparatively regarded as better than killing? Rachels finds that it is our experiences which compel us to feel that letting die is comparatively better than killing. It is a habit to learn from the news papers that most of the murders or direct killings are obviously horrific. On the other hand, we rarely hear about the incident of letting die except the work of doctors who are motivated to do this for humanitarian ground.

III.II.II ARGUMENT—III FROM REASONING

Another important point which has been raised by Rachels in order to treat the euthanasia whether it is active and passive, as same from the perspective of moral ground, lies in the fact that the doctors do nothing directly in case of passive euthanasia. What doctors do in case of passive euthanasia, in order to hasten the death of the terminal ill patients, is the withdrawal of the treatment. Withdrawing the treatment is a kind of decision taken by the doctors. Taking decision is no doubt to perform an act whose decision it may be. From this, it is clear that not to do something, is also a kind of doing something. So, here the doctors, in fact, do something directly though it has been explored as indirectly.

EUTHANASIA: A COMPARATIVE STUDY BETWEEN WESTERN AND INDIAN VIEWS

V. DIFFERENT TYPES OF EUTHANASIA LIKE CUSTOMS IN INDIA

From the Indian perspective, there is no such classification of euthanasia. But there are some religious centric deep seated customs which may be taken as euthanasia in some forms or others. The examples of such customs are *Santhara, Sati* or *Jauhar, Prayopavesa,* and *Mahasamadhi.* These are actually the spiritual paths through which the lives are to be sacrificed. In Indian culture, sacrificing lives through the spiritual ways are very common. In case of terminal disease or major disability a person can end his life in this way. In Indian perspective, though terminal illness leads to the death, it has been observed positively. Indian sages said that terminal illness is comparatively better than the accidental death which is sudden whereas the terminal illness gives some times when the patient may fulfil his incomplete works as far as possible. Again, the terminal ill patient can get the time of resuming his life. He has the opportunity to forgive those who hurt them as well as to take apologize from those who have been harassed by him in order to lead the life. In fact, terminal ill person get the time of self assessment in his life which helps him to end his life peacefully. Not only that, he can felt the dignity of life when he was free from any illness as well as at the time of his death.

Let us take a very brief account for these types of euthanasia like religious centric deep seated customs.

EUTHANASIA: A COMPARATIVE STUDY BETWEEN WESTERN AND INDIAN VIEWS

V.I SANTHARA

The custom *Santhara* is related to the Jain religion where it has been said that it is actually a way to achieve a peaceful and dignified death. It is believed that it welcomes the death of a person or helps in attaining self-awareness and spiritual freedom. It is evident that *Santhara* has been practiced since the establishment of Jainism which has also been reflected in their religious texts. *Santhara* is embedded in *Pratikraman* Sutra in *Shravaka Anuvrata*. It is the code of conduct of Jain followers. A person whose all purposes of life have been completed, or when the body of a Jain follower is not able to serve anymore, then a person is permitted to take the vow of *Santhara*. *Swetambara* Jain(s) calls it *Santhara*, whereas *Digambara* Jain(s) calls it *Sallekhana*.

Following Jain scriptures these are the conditions when a Jain follower can practice of *Santhara*:

- Falling into old age or suffering from a terminal disease from which deaths seems imminent.
- If there is any difficulty in performing normal physical functions due to some unknown reason.
- If the person fulfils all his responsibilities towards his family and society i.e. his mission of life has been completed.
- The person should take the decision for practicing *Santhara* without any pressure with a condition of good mental state and peace of mind.

EUTHANASIA: A COMPARATIVE STUDY BETWEEN WESTERN AND INDIAN VIEWS

- Before practicing *Santhara* the concerned person should take the permission from his family members and relatives.
- A firm conviction on his own decision.

Let it be noted that according to the Press Trust of India, an average number of 240 Jain(s) practice *Sallekhana* in each year in India.

The life is very precious to all of us, because life is such which can never be return, if it is lost. Human beings never like to loss his life. None can say that any terminal ill patient can never be cured in future. What human beings can think today can do it tomorrow. It may be the case that in future the term death will be removed from the dictionary. That is why there is a gap between taking a decision and the execution of that decision. When a Jain(s) takes a confirm decision going for *santhara*, he should follow some steps to execute his firm decision. These are as follows:

a. A person should practice regularly those duties which help him to keep the tranquillity of his mind through which his mind becomes to be prepared for the execution of *Santhara*.

b. He should take apologize from those who have been harmed by his actions willingly or unwillingly during his lifetime before performing this occasion.

c. He should review his decision again with the other saint of this religion.

EUTHANASIA: A COMPARATIVE STUDY BETWEEN WESTERN AND INDIAN VIEWS

d. He should practice deep meditation in order be contacted with his inner soul.

e. He then slowly and gradually restrains himself from food and water.

At last, his soul comes out of his body and his decision is executed.

V.II SATI OR JAUHAR

The meaning of the word 'sati' has been changed from time to time. The primary meaning of the term 'Sati' was surrounded in its reference to the goddess Sati who committed self-immolation, because her father *Dakṣa* insulted not only her but also Shiva, her husband. The term 'Sati' is used as a symbol of protest where one does not reluctant to accept death if he or she is disgraced. So, finally, sati means choosing death with self-respect rather than a life of humiliation.

The practice of Sati and committing suicide are not same, because their motives are different. The motive of sati is crystal clear—choosing death with self-respect rather than a life of humiliation whereas suicide has different motives.

Subsequently, the purpose of the Sati practice has been changed. During the *Chola* Empire, the Sati practice was aimed at gaining royal status where the basic criteria of sati i.e. the humiliating factor had been given importance. Sacrificing of life for husband was treated as the main factor. Later on, when India had been attacked by the Muslims and other foreign powers and defeated, especially the *Rajputs*, used to become

EUTHANASIA: A COMPARATIVE STUDY BETWEEN WESTERN AND INDIAN VIEWS

'Sati' in order to be escaped from rape, torture and dishonour. Though in the Ramayana, *Mandodari*, the wife of *Ravana*, or the wife of the Bali, did not become 'Sati' after the death of their husband. Rather they got married with their husband's brother, as they were not humiliated. [11]

In fact, sati was deeply rooted in the Hindu religious system. It was an amalgam of two distinct concepts: religious self-immolation and the burning of widows at their husbands' pyres. [12] Though these concepts are distinct concepts, these were common enough among many ancient tribes, and other primitive religious communities. Religious self-immolation is very important factor. That is why it was observed that in Mahabharata *Madri* decided to jump on the burning pyre of her husband *Pandu* as she was tremendously influenced by the guilty she felt in causing the death of her beloved husband. Due to the reverence of Self-immolation and 'death before dishonour principle' the *Rajput* queens used to follow the *Jahar Brata* when their husbands died in the battle field. And similar social conditions might have induced self-immolation as well as widow burning, in a male-dominated Hindu society, the chastity or purity of Widows became a prominent issue. But from present perspective each and every human being whether he is a man or woman must have the intrinsic value(i.e. right to life per se); and due to the right to life none is permitted to leave his or her life i.e. suicide is also a punishable offence.

V.III PRAYOPAVESA

Prayopavesa is a Hindu religious way through which a person can sacrifice his life with the help of uninterrupted fasting. In general, a religious person after preaching his religion, when he realizes that his mission has been completed can go for *Prayopavesa*. But a terminal ill patient can go for *Prayopavesa* also after taking consent from his family members as well as from his community. In order to finalize the decision, the family members can take the help of attorney which will be helpful not equalize the *Prayopavesa* with suicide or assisting suicide. Before execution the decision made by the concerned person, he must prepares his mind through a thorough review of his previous works and concentrating on the sacred scriptures as well as the teachings of the Guru. In the *Bhagavata Purana*, it was observed that *Parikshit*, the successor of the *Pandava*(s) sacrificed his life through *Prayopavesa*. *Vinayak Damodar Savarkar*, the great freedom fighter also went for *Prayopavesa* in 1966.

V.IV MAHASAMADHI

The word *Mahasamadhi* designates the final departure of the soul of a Yogi from his body. In case of ordinary human beings, after the death the soul also departs from the body, but the case of a Yogi is different, because in *Mahasamadhi*, the Yogi can depart the soul from his body the application of his Yogic power. In fact, when the death will come, we do not know; but the Yogi(s) know about the time of his death. Through the

EUTHANASIA: A COMPARATIVE STUDY BETWEEN WESTERN AND INDIAN VIEWS

deep meditation the Yogic(s) used to sacrifice their life. Sometimes, *Mahasamadhi* signifies the *para mukti* or *nirvikalpa* Samadhi. *Shyamacharan Lahiri Mahasaya*, who sacrificed his life through *Mahasamadhi* on 26th September, 1895.

Notes & References:

1. 'Euthanasia' means, according to the dictionary, 'a gentle and easy death', but it is now used to refer to the killing of those who are incurably ill and in great pain or distress, for the sake of those killed, and in order to spare them further suffering or distress. From—Singer, Peter: *Practical Ethics (2nd Ed.)*, Cambridge University Press, London, 2000, P— 175

2. Ibid. P—179

3. '...when the subject has never had the capacity to choose to live or die. From—Singer, Peter: *Practical Ethics (2nd Ed.)*, Cambridge University Press, London, 2000, P— 181

4. Involuntary euthanasia may be conducted when the person is incapable of making a decision and is thus left to a proxy. Euthanasia by proxy consent is a highly controversial subject, especially for the reason that multiple proxies may claim the authority to decide for the patient. From— Mohan, Dr. Vinitha: *Euthanasia: Ethical Implications* in *Prabuddha Bhrata*, Advaita Ashrama, Uttarakhand, Vol. 117, No. 8, August 2012, pp.412-4195.

5. Singer, Peter: *Practical Ethics (2nd Ed.)*, Cambridge University Press, London, 2000, P—201

6. Singer, Peter: *Practical Ethics (2nd Ed.)*, Cambridge University Press, London, 2000, P—201

7. Rachels, James: *Active and Passive Euthanasia*, Reprinted by permission of The New England Journal of Medicine, Vol. January 9, 1975, pp.78-80

8. Rachels, James: *Active and Passive Euthanasia*, Reprinted by permission of The New England Journal of Medicine, Vol. January 9, 1975, pp.78-80

9. Rachels, James: *Active and Passive Euthanasia*, Reprinted by permission of

EUTHANASIA: A COMPARATIVE STUDY BETWEEN WESTERN AND INDIAN VIEWS

The New England Journal of Medicine, Vol. January 9, 1975, pp.78-80

10. Rachels, James: *Active and Passive Euthanasia*, Reprinted by permission of The New England Journal of Medicine, Vol. January 9, 1975, pp.78-80

11. Gilmartin, Sophie: *The Sati, the Bride and the Widow: Sacrificial Woman in the Nineteenth Century*, Victorian Literature and Culture, Cambridge University Press, Vol. 25, Issue No. 1, 1997, P-141

12. Ganeri, Jonardon(Ed.): *The Collected Essays of Bimal Krishna Matilal Ethics and Epics*, Oxford University Press, New Delhi, 2002, P-154

> To destroy the boundary between healing and killing would mark a radical departure from longstanding legal and medical traditions of our country, posing a threat of unforeseeable magnitude to vulnerable members of our society. Those who represent the interests of elderly persons with disabilities, and persons with AIDS or other terminal illness, are justifiably alarmed when some hasten to confer on them "freedom": to be killed.—U.S. Catholic Bishop

CHAPTER: 3

Limitations of Euthanasia

CHAPTER: 3

Limitations of Euthanasia

Experience in the Netherlands, where there has been relatively little effort to improve pain and symptom treatment, suggests that legalization of physician assisted suicide might weaken society's resolve to expand services and resources aimed at caring for the dying patient. (Foley, 1995; Hendin, 1994)..."Treatment of Pain at the End of Life". A Position Statement from the American Pain Society

I. INTRODUCTION

Though in Chapter—2, different types of euthanasia and their justifications have been discussed, following Peter Singer; in order to find out the way through which the death could be dignified, we need more discussion on euthanasia from different perspectives. That is why this chapter will focus on a detail analysis cum evaluation on different types of Euthanasia. Though, in Indian context, there is no such term which can be used as a substitute of euthanasia, there are some activities which have been practiced in different cultures as well as in religions, from the past that may be taken as the alternative activities which are correlated to the euthanasia in Western Philosophical sense. Let it be noted that as the aim of this research work is to find out the best way to dignify the death, an analysis cum evaluation on euthanasia for anyone whether he is a terminal ill patient or not will be helpful to trace out the limitations of Euthanasia in Western sense and thereby to find out an alternative way. In order to search for the limitations, let

EUTHANASIA: A COMPARATIVE STUDY BETWEEN WESTERN AND INDIAN VIEWS

us make an analysis cum comparative approach between the arguments which are used in favour of euthanasia and the arguments which are used against euthanasia.

It has been mentioned earlier that the term euthanasia refers to the ending life of a person who has been suffering from some kind of terminal diseases which makes his life too much painful and miserable or in other words, leading the life for him or her is totally insignificant. Now, one may ask a problematic but justified question like this: how could one is to be confirmed that his or life is totally insignificant? As there are no fixed criteria through which the unworthy nature of leading a life could be determined, the meaning of the term euthanasia depends on some other auxiliary concepts. For example, none can, even a medical practitioner can say that any patient who has been in coma for a long time could not be revived in future. Naturally, the questions of legalization and the legitimization of euthanasia come again. That is why euthanasia has been morally preferred by all most all the countries, but not legalized as a public health policy by all. [1]Should euthanasia be allowed or not, if allowed which type of euthanasia, active or passive, is preferable? Which one, out of these two, should be prevailed? These are also the relevant questions which should also be addressed. Again, some of the supporters of euthanasia consider that the decision of the patients is very important, because human being can never be treated as means and he has an intrinsic value. In this case, the interest of the individual will outweigh. But the situation may like this: the individual who has been under unbearable pain for a long time, is not in a position to take any firm decision about his or her own death or in a coma, his or her interest will be hampered. In that case, the dignity of a society will be preferred. In fact, a dispute concerning the conflicts of interests i.e. the interest of the society; the interest of the individual and the interest of the government are to be entertained. One may cast doubt about the interest of the government regarding euthanasia. In fact, this is a public policy, that's why the interest of the government must be involved.

II. OBSERVATIONS ON THE ARGUMENTS FOR EUTHANASIA

Though euthanasia has not been accepted by many countries legally as a public health policy; it has some positive features which means there are some grounds through which euthanasia can be supported. These grounds are the juxtaposition of some arguments based on Effective Evidences and some are based on Case Studies. Among these two types of arguments, the foremost positive features for euthanasia have been emerged out of moral perspective. Euthanasia, at least from moral perspective, should be supported, because it is one of the ways to give relieve patient from the intolerably extreme pain and suffering. It also relieves the terminally ill people from a lingering death. In fact, each and every human being like to lead a dignified life, life without any dignity, is unworthy. Going against euthanasia implies the restriction of freedom of choice of the individual. Euthanasia being a moral issue, dignifies the

EUTHANASIA: A COMPARATIVE STUDY BETWEEN WESTERN AND INDIAN VIEWS

choice of a person which is a fundamental principle. Though, it has been mentioned earlier that euthanasia as a public health policy has not been approved by most of the countries. A public health policy is not just only the matter of ethics; it depends on many factors such as economical condition, cultural frame work, health infrastructures, different types of social values etc. Let us discuss some of the arguments from the perspective of Effective Arguments in order to support euthanasia.

II.I.I EFFECTIVE EVIDENCE ARGUMENT (EEA-1) ON MEDICAL GROUND

Some moral philosophers argue for euthanasia in the ground that medical facilities for the most of developing countries are limited. That's why when a patient gives his or her consent in favour of euthanasia, in order to get relive from his or her long terminal illness; it is the duty of the state to consider his or her choice. In that case, the other patients could get the opportunity to have the medical facilities. In other words, keeping in mind the limitation of providing the treatment, it can be said from the perspective of the fair innings argument [2] that it is the duty of the state to provide the medical facilities for those who are young and could be recovered soon instead of giving medical facilities for those who are old and there are least possibilities to be recovered soon.

II.I.II EEA—2 ON THE BASSIS OF THE DIGNITY OF LIFE

The article 21 of the Indian Constitution talks about the life with dignity. This article clearly states that a person has a right

EUTHANASIA: A COMPARATIVE STUDY BETWEEN WESTERN AND INDIAN VIEWS

to live a life having minimum dignity and he or she should be given the right to choice to end his or her life when he or she has been living under minimum dignity. Supporters of euthanasia also argue in favour of Active Euthanasia as like as Passive Euthanasia which has already been allowed by the country. A patient should be given the right to choice the end of his or her life through a painless death, in order to be get relief from excessive agony rather than living a miserable life with severe pain and suffering. Thus, from the basis of the dignity of life, a terminal ill patient should be allowed for euthanasia.

II.I.III EEA—3 ON THE GROUND OF RIGHT TO DIE

'Right-to-die' supporters argue that people who have an incurable, degenerative, disabling or debilitating condition should be allowed to die in dignity. This argument is further defended for those, who have chronic debilitating illness even though it is not terminal such as severe mental illness. Majority of such petitions are filed by the sufferers or family members or their caretakers. The caregiver's burden is huge and cuts across various domains such as financial, emotional, time, physical, mental and social. Hence, it is not uncommon to hear requests from the family members of the person with psychiatric illness to give some poison either to patient or else to them. In fact, when the life is coupled with the states inefficiency, apathy and no investment on health it is nothing but mockery to demand the 'Right to life'. In this situation 'Right to die' seems to be more preferable than 'Right to life'.

EUTHANASIA: A COMPARATIVE STUDY BETWEEN WESTERN AND INDIAN VIEWS

II.I.IV EEA—4 REFUSING ANY MEDICAL TREATMENT

Right to refuse any kind of medical treatment is a well established law. A patient, for example, who has been suffering from blood cancer, can refuse to take any kind of medical facilities or deny consuming food through naso-gastric tube. Acknowledgement of the right to refuse the treatment by the patient is actually signifies Passive Euthanasia. Denying or termination of any kind of medical treatment before 16 weeks of pregnancy is also another kind of Active Involuntary Euthanasia. Holland discussed seriously the issue of mercy killing of deformed babies.

II.I.V EEA—5 EQUAL IMPORTANCE ON RIGHT TO LIFE AND DEATH

'Right to life' and 'right to die' should be taken as the two sides of the same coin when a person is in vegetative stage or in a chronic illness. Being a member of a family, a chronic ill patient may prefer the economic stability of his or her family without taking any treatment. He or she may think not to be the burden on his or her family. Euthanasia can give the opportunity to the terminal ill patient to keep intact the stable condition of his family through the fulfilment of 'right to die.' Again, the option—'right to die' through euthanasia can be turn into the 'right to life' for some patients who need badly the organic transplantation.

EUTHANASIA: A COMPARATIVE STUDY BETWEEN WESTERN AND INDIAN VIEWS

II.I.VI EEA—6 PROTECTION OF LIFE

'Right to life', following the constitution of India, runs towards the positive direction—the protection of life. Food, safe drinking water and health care are the minimum needs of protecting life in the earth which should be provided by any state to its citizens in every condition whatever it may be. But, most of the countries, due to huge population, failed to provide sufficient food, shelter, education, health care etc. which are the basic needs for survival amongst the normal citizens. That's why terminal ill persons who have been appealing for euthanasia their prayer should be considered seriously for granting the euthanasia.

II.I.VII EEA—7 DUTY TO RELIF FROM MISERY

It is a fact that sufferings at the end of life, is sometimes so unavoidable and unbearable that it deserve a duty to help the people to give relief from such kind of misery. This could be possible if and only if physicians are free to prescribe the assisted suicide. Nonetheless, the doctor should be reassured more than one time before making such type of prescription which is linked with the death of a human being. However, the situation is different. Much time and money have been spent in order to keep alive the terminal ill and/or coma patient which is actually damaging the society. [3]

EUTHANASIA: A COMPARATIVE STUDY BETWEEN WESTERN AND INDIAN VIEWS

II.I.VIII EEA—8 OBSERVATION OF THE OPINION OF DESMOD TUTU

It is an argument put forwarded by Desmond Tutu, ThM, who is the South African Anglican Archbishop Emeritus, for favouring assisted dying. His argument is very straight forward. He argued, if the constitution of South Africa assures the dignity of human right through the laws, then the right of any South African citizen should be protected by these laws. But the actual situation is different when he came to learn that Craig *Schonegevel* committed suicide on 1st September, 2009 after swallowing 12 sleeping pills and covering his heads with two plastic bags with elastic band. He had to commit suicide on the ground that his quality of life became too much poor as (i) he had to undergo many surgical processes, (ii) he had to bear intolerable pain, (iii) he had been struggling for 28 years, (iv) no improvement was observed after the treatment, (v) no legal decision was taken for assisted killing. Tutu added that Craig *Schonegevel* could have die in the laps of his beloved parent Patsy and Neville, listening his favourite music, if he was permitted to end his life legally assisted what he wanted for. In fact, his last choice was not considered, either from the humanitarian ground or from the legal ground, though the constitution of South Africa has the provision of dignity of human right. In fact, the dignity of human right is associated with the dignity of the free choice of the individual citizen of the country. That's why Tutu remarked, 'I revere the sanctity of life – but not at any cost. I confirm I don't want my life prolonged. I can see I would probably incline towards the quality of life argument, whereas others will be more comfortable with palliative care. Yes, I think a lot of people would be upset if I said I wanted assisted dying. I would say I wouldn't mind actually.' [4]

II.I.IX EEA—9 ARGUMENT PUT FORWARDED BY MICHEL IRWIN

Michael Irwin, former Medical Director at the United Nations and current Coordinator of the Society for Old Age Rational Suicide (SOARS) argues for euthanasia, from the perspective of personal choice i.e. right to die should be a matter of personal choice. Personal choice of a person should be extended up to the end of life, because we are free to choice about what we learn, what we work, whom we marry etc. At the edge of our life we should be given free hand for the choice of death. He said, 'I'm pro life – I want to live as long as I possibly can, but I also believe the law should be changed to let anyone with some severe medical condition which is causing unbearable symptoms to have an assisted suicide. I wouldn't want to be unnecessarily kept alive against my own will.' [5]

II.I.X EEA—10 ARGUMENT OF STEPHEN HAWKING

Stephen Hawking also favours euthanasia. He argues that being human we are permitted to give the relief from pain to the animals by killing when some animals suffer. Similarly, when someone appeals for assisted suicide in a fully self conscious state, in order to get relief from intolerable pains, he or she must be given favourable consideration. To quote Hawking,

> 'I think those who have a terminal illness and are in great pain should have the right to choose to end their lives and those that help them should be free from prosecution. We don't let animals suffer, so why humans?' [6]

II.I.XI EEA—11 ARGUMENT BY MARICA ANGELL

Being a doctor, a Senior Lecturer in Social Medicine at Harvard Medical School and the former Editor-in-Chief of New England Journal of Medicine, Marcia Angell argued in an article 'May Doctors Help You to Die?' published in *New York Review of Books* on October 11, 2012 in favour of euthanasia. He said that the ground for the legalization of euthanasia should not be based only on the active nature of the doctors. In fact, treatment is two ways traffic. Both the choices of the doctors and the patients deserve the same dignity and priority. If the patient is inactive and the doctor is active, there will be no fruitful result but the wastage time, money and energy. 'When healing is no longer possible, when death is imminent and patients find their suffering unbearable', Marcia Angell said, 'then the physician's role should shift from healing to relieving suffering in accord with the patient's wishes.'

II.I.XII EEA—12 ARGUMENT OF JACKSON KEVORKIAN

Jack Kevorkian, a retired pathologist known as 'Dr. Death', because of assisting 130 people to end their lives argues for euthanasia in an interview (1990) with *Cornerstone* magazine.

EUTHANASIA: A COMPARATIVE STUDY BETWEEN WESTERN AND INDIAN VIEWS

He said that the aged persons who are healthy and mentally competent, but not in any kind of depression, has a right for suicide, because a person has a right to determine what will or will not be done to his body.

These are the arguments based on effective evidences. Let us analyse some arguments which are based on Case Studies for euthanasia.

II.II.I ARGUMENT FROM CASE STUDY—1

David *Goodall,* an Australian botanist and ecologist chose to end his life via Voluntary Euthanasia in a Swiss clinic on May 10, 2018 at the age of 104, put forwarded arguments for his decision in an interview before his death as follows:

Up to the age of 90, I was enjoying life, but not now. It has passed by me, and I have done the best I can with it. My abilities and eyesight are declining, and I no longer want to live this way. I am happy to have this opportunity [physician-assisted suicide], which I call the Swiss option. I hope something positive will come out of my story and that other countries will adopt a more liberal view of assisted suicide. I'd like to be remembered as an instrument for freeing the elderly to choose their own death. [7]

II.II.II ARGUMENT FROM CASE STUDY—2

The other case study has been advocated by Annette Childs, a psychotherapist, in the article, *Nevada's Death with Dignity Bill Would Ease Fears: Annette Childs* published in May

18, 2017 (www.rgi.com). In this article, the author explores the psychological factors concerned with the death for an aged person who is in the verge of his death. He explains how the fear of death is terrific than death itself. The modern powerful medicine is, however, liable in giving relief the patient from the physical sufferings. But the psychological sufferings are the most worst. 'It is called anticipatory suffering, and it includes the depression and anxiety that accompanies fear of death and fear of what is believed to be the inevitable suffering that comes with end of life. Death is perhaps the most personal intimate event of any lifetime—and fear is a horrible form of suffering. For those who fear a prolonged and/or suffering death, this type of legislation provides a potent medicine. Opponents focus on the actual end of life medications and how they could be misused, when the thing we may be better served to focus on is the placebo effect that occurs for those who never take the medications—but find their suffering relieved by the simple knowing that they have a choice.'

II.II.III ARGUMENT FROM CASE STUDY—3

In California, physician assisted suicide has been legalized by the Governor Jerry Brown since October 15, 2015. Jerry Brown nicely represented his position about euthanasia. Being a Governor, he read all the arguments for and against euthanasia. Primarily, it seems to be a crime, because human beings still now failed to give life of a death person. In other words, life is not just a product of laboratory. But after a careful scrutiny of the opinions put forwarded by the doctors, religious leaders, general citizens and the heartfelt petition made by from Brittany Maynard's family and Archbishop Desmond Tutu; he signed in favour of physician-assisted suicide in California.

II.II.IV ARGUMENT FROM CASE STUDY—4

It was a case study of Brittany Maynard, a 29-year old woman who had been suffering with stage 4 *Glioblastoma multiforme* (a malignant brain tumour) launched a campaign with Compassion & Choices to raise awareness about Death with Dignity laws, before her death by taking lethal medication prescribed by her doctors in Oregon on November 1, 2014. She argued that she wanted to live but, *Glioblastoma* was going to kill her which was out of control her. Out of control means, any medicine was impotent to cure her. At this stage she felt herself helpless, unbearable and terrifying. She thought if she had a switch in her body which allow for suicide she must switched on it. She remarked,

> I've discussed with many experts how I would die from it, and it's a terrible, terrible way to die. Being able to choose to go with dignity is less terrifying... Right now it's a choice that's only available to some Americans, which is really unethical... The amount of sacrifice and change my family had to go through in order to get me legal access to Death with Dignity–changing our residency [from California to Oregon], establishing a team of doctors, having a place to live–was profound... There's tons of Americans who don't have time or the ability or finances [to move to a legal state] and I don't think that's right or fair... I believe this choice is ethical, and what makes it ethical is it is a choice. [8]

EUTHANASIA: A COMPARATIVE STUDY BETWEEN WESTERN AND INDIAN VIEWS

III. OBSERVATIONS ON THE ARGUMENTS AGAINST EUTHANASIA

Some countries still now do not permit euthanasia legally. Human being is the top among the all species in the world. Through the emergence of his inner power, human being has changed the way of evolution in the earth. For him, nothing is impossible. What he can think today, he can do tomorrow. The diseases which are regarded as terminal or incurable today, it may be curable tomorrow. Today the transplantation of heart, kidneys, lever, cornea etc. is possible. Even suddenly detached hand or leg can be joined by surgery. That is why it is natural to go against euthanasia. Life is such a precious God gifted authority which can never be returned.

Let us analysis some of the arguments against euthanasia which are based on reason. Among these reason based arguments, the religious argument: euthanasia can never be justified from the perspective of a religious person, because of the religious faith on God that only God has the right to end a human life; the 'slippery slope' argument: this is based on the fact that if euthanasia is legalised then it could lead to significant unintended changes in our healthcare system and society at large that we would later come to regret; the medical ethics argument: asking doctors, nurses or any other health professional to carry out acts of euthanasia or assist in a suicide would not only be a violation of fundamental medical ethics, but also the violation of the Hippocratic Oath— I will give no deadly medicine to any one if asked, nor suggest any counsel; and the alternative argument: there is no reason a person should suffer either mentally or physically as there are effective end-of-life treatments available, so euthanasia is not a valid treatment option but instead represents a failure on the part of the doctor involved in a person's care are best.

III.I THE RELIGIOUS ARGUMENT

The most common religious argument against euthanasia is that human beings are the sacred creation of God, so human life is by extension sacred. This means there must a limitation on what humans can do with their life, such as ending it. Only God has the power to end a human life, so committing an act of euthanasia or assisting in suicide is acting against the will of God and is sinful. This argument, or variations on it, is shared by the Christian, Jewish and Islamic faiths.

In this argument it is also said that the human life is a gift of God; human beings are not capable of giving life, that's why he or she has no authority to take life. Even none can free to decide to give up or sacrifice his or her life, in the name of euthanasia. Taking life is totally wrong and irreligious. Only God has the power to take life and no human being has the right to act as a God. Euthanasia actually devalues human life.

III.II THE SLIPPERY SLOPE ARGUMENT

The slippery slope argument is rest upon the idea that once the euthanasia is granted by a state along with the positive consent of the healthcare service; this signifies that a border line is crossed which should have never been crossed and a

EUTHANASIA: A COMPARATIVE STUDY BETWEEN WESTERN AND INDIAN VIEWS

dangerous precedent has been set. In this case, a society that allows Voluntary Euthanasia will then gradually change its attitudes to include non-voluntary and then involuntary euthanasia. Legalised euthanasia, could eventually lead to a wide range of unforeseen consequences, such as the following:

➢ Very ill people who need constant care or people with severe disabilities may feel pressured to request euthanasia so they are not a burden to their family.

➢ Legalizing euthanasia may discourage research into palliative treatments and possibly cures for people with terminal illnesses.

➢ Doctors may occasionally be badly mistaken about a patient's diagnosis and outlook and the patient may chose euthanasia as they have been wrongly told they have a terminal condition.

III.III MEDICAL ETHICS ARGUMENT

The medical ethics argument states that legalisation of euthanasia would violate one of the most important laws in medical ethics, which in the words of the International Code of Medical Ethics is: 'A doctor must always bear in mind the obligation of preserving human life from conception.'

Asking doctors to abandon their obligation to preserve human life could fatally damage the doctor-patient relationship. Doctors could become hardened to death and the process of causing death becomes a routine administrative task. This could lead to a lack of compassion when dealing with elderly, disabled or terminally ill patients.

In turn, people with complex health needs or severe disabilities could become distrustful of their doctor's efforts and intentions, thinking their doctor would rather 'kill them off' than take responsibility for a complex and demanding case.

III.IV THE ALTERNATIVE ARGUMENT

The alternative argument says that euthanasia is not at all the substitute of any medical treatment whatever it may be. It actually discloses the limitation cum failure of the medical treatment. Human being has the enormous power. He can do anything. What he can think today can do tomorrow. When any patient seeks euthanasia, after the failure of the doctors, this means the doctors are given an escape route to fulfil the gap in their profession. If a patient asks for dignified death through euthanasia, he or she is actually dishonouring the medical profession. That's why, the doctors should always be pessimistic and there any kind of euthanasia must be disallowed.

III.V ARGUMENT FROM LEGALIZATION

We have learned earlier that euthanasia as a moral rule has been accepted by almost all countries, but it has not been legalized by many countries in the ground that 'right to life' is a natural right which has been embodied in the constitution of a country. Such as the Article 21 of Indian constitution goes against any type of suicide or an unnatural termination or extinction of life as it is incompatible and inconsistent with the concept of 'right to life'. It is the duty of the state to protect life of its citizens and it is the duty of the physicians to provide care without doing any harm to the patients. If euthanasia is legalised, then one may caste doubt about the duty of the state regarding the health which should be performed. It will be a grave apprehension that the state may refuse to invest in health i.e. to protect the Right to life. Legalised euthanasia may lead to a severe decline in the quality of appropriate care for terminally-ill patients. Hence, in a welfare state there should not be any role of euthanasia in any form.

III.VI ARGUMENT FROM CONFLICT INTERESTS

In this era of declining morality and justice, there is a possibility of misusing euthanasia by family members or relatives for inheriting the property of the patient. It has been reflected in the recent judgments of the Supreme Court also. 'Mercy killing' should not lead to 'killing mercy' in the hands of the noble medical practitioners. Hence, to keep control over the medical professionals, the Indian Medical Council in its Regulations, 2002 has also discusses euthanasia sincerely in Chapter 6, Section 6.7. There is an urgent need to protect patients and also medical practitioners caring the terminally ill patients from unnecessary lawsuit.

III.VII ARGUMENT FROM THE CARE

Earlier, majority of the patients used to die before they reached the hospital, but now the scenario has been changed, because of the huge advancement of medical science. Now, life can be prolonged, but not to that extent of bringing back the dead one. Earlier, diseases results were considered in terms of 'CURE' but now the diseases such as cancer, aids, diabetes, hypertension and mental illness are talked about in terms of best 'CARE'. The principle is now—to add life to years, rather than years to life with a good quality Palliative Care. The intention is to provide care when cure is not possible by low cost methods. The expectation of society is, 'cure' from the health professionals, but the role of medical professionals is to provide 'care'. Hence, euthanasia for incurable illness does not based on a solid logical argument. Whenever, there is no cure, the society and medical professionals become frustrated and the fellow citizens take extreme measures such as euthanasia. In such situations, palliative and rehabilitative care comes to the rescue of the patient and the family. At times, doctors do suggest to the family members to have the patient discharged from the hospital wait for death to come, if the family or patient so desires. Euthanasia should never be encouraged.

III.VIII ARGUMENT OF PROFESSION

It is the duty of the doctors to save the life of the patients. Euthanasia whether it is passive or active, discloses the limitation cum failure of the medicinal treatment. Every profession has its own limitation, but accepting euthanasia may go against the profession of the doctors. The doctors may avoid resolving the critical diseases, if euthanasia is granted. Again, the poor patients and their family members may refuse or

EUTHANASIA: A COMPARATIVE STUDY BETWEEN WESTERN AND INDIAN VIEWS

withdraw treatment because of the huge cost involved in keeping them alive, if euthanasia is legalized. Furthermore, if euthanasia is supported by the law, then commercial health sector will serve death sentence to many disabled and elderly citizens for meagre amount of money.

Through research it has been approved that many terminally ill patients requesting euthanasia with having major depression, and the neglecting attitudes take by the other members of the family towards the patient. In fact, these patients need palliative and rehabilitative care. They want to be looked after by enthusiastic, compassionate and humanistic team of health professionals and the complete expenses need to be borne by the State so that 'Right to life' becomes a reality and succeeds before 'Right to death with dignity'. In fact, euthanasia is totally against the medical ethics, and public health policy. It is the task of Medical ethics how to provide the patients for nursing, care giving and healing, but not ending the life of the patient. Present day, medical science reaches its top position. Some diseases which were seemed to be incurable in the past are now becoming curable. Thus, instead of encouraging a patient to end his life, the medical practitioners should encourage the patients to lead their painful life with strength.

The above mentioned view has also been supported by

(i) The American College of Physicians. They said,

> On the basis of substantive ethics, clinical practice, policy, and other concerns articulated in this position paper, the ACP does not

EUTHANASIA: A COMPARATIVE STUDY BETWEEN WESTERN AND INDIAN VIEWS

support legalization of physician-assisted suicide. It is problematic given the nature of the patient–physician relationship, affects trust in the relationship and in the profession, and fundamentally alters the medical profession's role in society. Furthermore, the principles at stake in this debate also underlie medicine's responsibilities regarding other issues and the physician's duties to provide care based on clinical judgment, evidence, and ethics. Society's focus at the end of life should be on efforts to address suffering and the needs of patients and families, including improving access to effective hospice and palliative care. [9]

(ii) George Delgado, MD, Medical Director and family practice physician at Culture of Life Family Care. He remarked,

> Physician-assisted suicide does damage to patients who are in very difficult situations. It does damage to the medical profession. It compromises the sacred trust between physician and patient, which should be based on healing, not based on killing. [9]

(iii) Richard *Doerflinger*, MA, Public Policy Fellow at the University of Notre Dame's Centre for Ethics and Culture supported by saying,

> Campaigning to end certain people's lives doesn't end suffering – it passes on the suffering to other similar people, who now have to fear they are the next people in line to be seen as having worthless lives. And people who have died from a drug overdose have no freedom of choice at all. Moreover, societies that authorize suicide as a 'choice' for some people soon end up placing pressure on them to 'do the right thing' and kill themselves... Seeing suicide as a solution for some illnesses can only undermine the willingness of doctors and society to learn how to show real compassion and address patients' pain and other problems. In states that have legalized assisted suicide, in fact, most patients request the lethal drugs not due to

EUTHANASIA: A COMPARATIVE STUDY BETWEEN WESTERN AND INDIAN VIEWS

pain (or even fear of future pain), but due to concerns like 'loss of dignity' and 'becoming a burden on others' – attitudes that these laws encourage. The solution is to care for people in ways that assure them that they have dignity and it is a privilege, not a burden, to care for them as long as they live. [10]

III.IX ARGUMENT FROM THE BURDEN TO SOCIETY

The decision of euthanasia, in general, is not taken solely by the patient. Many persons are involved to finalize such kind of crucial decision. The relatives of patient sometimes pay an important role in order to take the final decision. Hence, it is probable that the patient comes under the pressure and takes such a drastic step of ending life. Of course, in such cases the pressure is not physical, it is rather moral and psychological which proves to be much stronger. The patient himself starts to feel that he is a burden on the relatives when they take such a decision for him and finally he also succumbs to it. To some extent it is applicable to the other groups of more vulnerable people. There is a risk of acceptance of euthanasia by all of them simply in the ground that they are nothing but the burden to society.

III.X ARGUMENT OF NON-REPLACE-ABILITY

In order to justify non-voluntary euthanasia, Peter Singer says, one may not oppose euthanasia when it is applied to the physically and mentally disable infants, on the ground that they are not capable to protect their right to live in any form. Only a few parents, from the perspective of natural tendency of love towards their children, may not accept euthanasia. But from the aspect of 'total' version of utilitarianism [11] euthanasia for the physically and mentally disable children may be granted. A parent may plan to have another fit child after the non existence of unfit child. In that case, Peter Singer says, replace-ability argument will not permit to do that; because human children are not replaceable.

IV. CONCLUSION

Though Aristotle defines human being as a rational animal, the manifestations of rationality for human beings are not similar. That is why some human beings are called as genius who can transcendent their time. They are eligible to frame such policies which help the human beings to reign in this planet for a long time. Euthanasia is truly that type of public health policy which goes ahead of the time. It is morally permissible, but its legalization depends on the enlightenment of the entire human species.

Notes & References:

1. Similarly, the judgment that an act is morally acceptable does not imply that the law should permit it. For example, the belief that euthanasia is morally justified for terminally ill infants who faces uncontrollable pain and suffering is consistent with the belief that the government should legally prohibit such euthanasia on grounds that it should not be possible to control abuses if it is legalized.—Beauchamp, Tom, L & Childress, James, F: *Principles of Biomedical Ethics*, Oxford University Press, New York, 2013, P-10

2. Fair innings argument: This argument reflects the idea that everyone is entitled to some "normal" span of life years. According to this argument,

younger persons have stronger claims to life- saving interventions than older persons because they have had fewer opportunities to experience life (5). The implication is that saving one year of life for a young person is valued more than saving one year of life for an older person. From Ethical considerations in developing a public health response to pandemic influenza, WHO/CDS/EPR/GIP/2007.2, P-5

3. "Certainly, suffering at the end of life is sometimes unavoidable and unbearable, and helping people end their misery may be necessary. Given the opportunity, I would support laws to provide these kinds of [physician-assisted suicide] prescriptions to people. About half don't even use their prescription. They are reassured just to know they have this control if they need it. But we damage entire societies if we let providing this capability divert us from improving the lives of the ill." by Atul Gawande, MD, MPH, Surgeon at Brigham and Women's Hospital, in his book, *Being Mortal*, 2014.

4. Tutu, Desmond: *Desmond Tutu: A Dignified Death Is Our Right – I Am in Favour of Assisted Dying*, July, 2014

5. Irwin, Michael: *Euthanasia: The Right to Die Should Be a Matter of Personal Choice*, August, 2013

6. Interview of Stephen Hawking with the BBC on September 17, 2013, www.bbc.com

7. Bachmann, Helena & Stanglin, Doug: David Goodall, 104, Takes Final Journey at Swiss Assisted-Suicide Clinic, May, 2018, www. usatoday.com

8. *People* magazine article, Oct. 6, 2014, www.people.com

9. In National Catholic Reporter article, 'Judge OKs Court Challenge to California's Assisted Suicide Law', June 20, 2017, https://ncronline.org

10. In Charlotte Lozier Institute interview, 'Q&A with the Scholars: Physician-Assisted Suicide and Euthanasia' available at the Lozier Institute website

11. This expression is used by Peter Singer, in his book, *Practical Ethics*, Cambridge University Press, New York, 2000, P-185

EUTHANASIA: A COMPARATIVE STUDY BETWEEN WESTERN AND INDIAN VIEWS

> Not all moral issues have same moral weight as abortion and euthanasia. There may be a legitimate diversity of opinion even among Catholics about waging war and applying the death penalty but not ...with regard to abortion and euthanasia.—Pope Benedict XVI

CHAPTER: 4

Some Other Theories and Their Limitations

CHAPTER: 4

Some Other Theories and Their Limitations

The ideal man bears the accidents of life with dignity and grace, making the best of circumstances.—Aristotle

I. INTRODUCTION

In the last chapter i.e. in chapter-3, it has been mentioned that there is no term in Indian context which can be taken at par with the meaning of Euthanasia, but there are several customs cum activities which are followed by some of the Indian people to make the death as dignified as possible. Among these sacred customs cum activities, *Santhara*, *Sati* or *Jauhar*, *Prayopavesa*, and *Mahasamadhi* are significant. Nonetheless, it should be mentioned that in India passive Euthanasia has been legalized by the Supreme Court based on some acute conditions. Before the deliberations on some other theories which are concerned with the euthanasia and/or to dignify the death directly or indirectly such as palliative care, life prolonging treatment, hospice service, telling the obvious truth and so on from Western perspective and *Santhara*, *Sati* or *Jauhar*, *Prayopavesa*, *Mahasamadhi* and so on from the Indian perspective, let us peep in to the (i) background of the legal implementation of passive Euthanasia in India through the verdict of Supreme Court and (ii) the relation among suicide, homicide and euthanasia.

II. BACKGROUND OF THE LEGAL IMPLEMENTATION OF PASSIVE EUTHANASIA IN INDIA

Aruna Shanbaug, a nurse at King Edward Memorial Hospital, Mumbai became blind, paralysed, speechless and irreversible coma patient after a terrifying done by a ward boy on the night of November 27th, 1973. She had been cared by King Edward Memorial Hospitalnurses and doctors for a long period though she didn't want to live any more as the doctors failed to show any scope of recovery. When *Pinki Virani*, her 'next friend' (a legal term used for a person speaking on behalf of someone who is incapacitated) discovered her as—'her bones are brittle. Her skin is like 'Paper Mache' stretched over a skeleton. Her wrists are twisted inwards; her fingers are bent and fisted towards her palms, resulting in growing nails tearing into the flesh very often. Her teeth are decayed and giving her immense pain. Food is given to her in semisolid form. She chokes on liquids and is in a persistent vegetative state.' immediately moved to the Supreme Court with a plea to direct the said Hospital not to force her for feeding but to end her life i.e. the implementation of Euthanasia and on 16th December 2009, the Supreme Court of India admitted the plea for the end of life of her client. A special bench comprising of Chief Justice K. G.*Balakrishnan*, Justices A. K.*Ganguly* and B. S.*Chauhan,* after the order of the Supreme Court agreed to examine the merits of the petition and sought responses from the Union

EUTHANASIA: A COMPARATIVE STUDY BETWEEN WESTERN AND INDIAN VIEWS

Government, Commissioner of Mumbai Police and Dean of KEM Hospital.

On 24th January 2011, the Supreme Court of India responded to the plea for euthanasia filed by *PinkiVirani*, after setting up a three-members medical committee. On the basis of the recommendations of the medical committee, the Supreme Court in its verdict allowed Passive Euthanasia in India by laying out the guidelines for Passive Euthanasia i.e. the withdrawing of treatment or food that would allow the patient to die.

It is a fact that the verdict announced by the Supreme Court on the basis of the appeal forwarded by *PinkiVirani* for Ms. Shanbaug changed forever India's approach to the contentious issue of euthanasia, because the other Indians are now eligible to argue in court for the right to withhold medical treatment i.e. take a patient off a ventilator, for example, in the case of an irreversible coma or in persistent vegetative state. [1]

III. SUICIDE, HOMICIDE, EUTHANASIA & ASSISTED SUCIDE

However, Euthanasia is totally different from suicide and homicide. Attempt to commit suicide is punishable offence under section 309 of IPC and abetment to suicide is punishable under section 306 of IPC. A person commits suicide for various reasons like marital discord, dejection of love, failure in the examination, unemployment etc. But in case of euthanasia, these reasons do not carry any importance. Suicide is purely private and depends on the decision of the individual person who is supposed to commit suicide, whereas, Euthanasia is public. Euthanasia means putting a person to painless death who has been suffering from incurable diseases or when the life becomes purposeless or hopeless due to prolonged mental or physical handicap situation. It is also differs from homicide. In murder, the murderer has the intention to cause harm or cause death in his mind. But in euthanasia, although there is an intention to cause of the death, but such intention is emerged out of good faith. A doctor applies euthanasia only when the patient has been suffering from a terminal disease. The intention of the doctor is very much clear—it is the permanent relief from the irreversible sufferings. [2]

IV. SOME OTHER WAYS HOW TO DIGNIFY THE DEATH FROM WESTERN PERSPECTIVE

It is true that death is eternal. No created animal has the power of avoiding death. Human, being rational not only honoured by the right to life but also tries to make his or her death dignified. Euthanasia, being one of the best morally accepted ways of ending life for the terminal ill patients, have failed to secure the guaranty of the dignity of death as it is still treated as one of the most debatable issue of life and death. In fact, the terminal illness deserves terminal care which cannot be available through treatments that are provided in the hospitals, as the numbers of seats in the hospitals are limited. Terminal care is a kind of special treatment which is applied for those who are in the verge of death due to the routine incurable illness. It includes financial, social, psychological, spiritual, physical and mental assistance. The availability of medical care is an important and influential concern for a terminal ill patient. Terminal care for the elderly persons, give relief physical and mental pain by installing hope in the mind. [3] Through terminal care, they start to think that their lives are not valueless due to their age or routine illness though their lives are not so financially secured. In fact, the aged persons fail to think rationally that they should not be afraid of death; physical pain is very common at that old age and there is no strong relationship between pain and immediate death. It is the terminal care, through which the aged persons can get the guidance how to think positively at the old age, even at verge of death. Being a part of life, illness may increase anxiety and fear, but life should be enjoyed whether it is in old age or it is in a crisis. That is why let us consider some of the ways which are used to dignify the death of the patient in addition to Euthanasia.

IV.I PALLIATIVE CARE

Care for the relief of physical pain of the patient who does not response the medical treatment in the hospital due to the old age or terminal illness, may be referred to the total active care unit which is also known as Palliative Care. Therapeutic treatments are often a combination of more invasive and radical approaches which involve the use of drugs and include surgical invasive or semi-invasive procedures. This type of treatment generates some side effects and toxicityinto the patient's body. Naturally, this method is somehow risky, expensive as well as limited application.Furthermore, healing may require frequent intervention and intensive monitoring which generates panic to the aged persons. The mere necessity of repeated clinical visits or hospitalizations is annoying. On the other hand, palliative care seeks to alleviate the symptoms of the disease without any healing effect. The main goal of Palliative Care is to achieve the best possible quality of life for the patient and the patient's family. Palliative Care treatment involves the control of pain and other symptoms. Medications may be needed to relieve physical symptoms such as shortness of breath, insomnia, anxiety, depression etc. otherwise, other methods may be used. However, the palliative care can never be considered as an alternative to healing. This treatment is recommended only when all possible cares are considered or seems to be failed. This treatment is mostly applied for those patients who have advanced stage of cancer. In a nutshell, the concept of palliative care reassures faith in life, even though death is a normal process. Its purpose is to relieve annoying symptoms. [4]

It is mistakenly believed that palliative care is unscientific and helps to speed up the process of death. Such a belief is completely baseless. When a patient has been suffering from a routine illness, the death will occur naturally. Palliative Care teaches the patients how toenjoy the last days of life after averting the fear of death.Palliative Care takes a multidisciplinary approach. This approach includes emotional, social and spiritual. This is not just for the patient; it is for the support of the whole family.

IV.II LIFE PROLONGING TREATMENTS

Advanced technology in modern times, introduced entirely new way for life care, through which lifespan can be prolonged and death may be postponed, for the time being. Transplantation therapy of organs has challenged the concept of incurability. We can no more define a disease as permanently incurable as there is always a chance of organic replace-ability or invention of new lifegiving medicines. The progressive diseases like chronic renal failure, respiratory problem, cardiac and liver failure, leukaemia and other blood cancers are now treated as curable, instead of incurable. 'Sometimes, literally speaking, life is brought back from the jaws of death with the help of life prolonging treatments like assisted respirator support, artificial maintenance of nutrition and hydration cardiac pacing and so on.'[5]

IV.III HOSPICE SERVICES

Hospice service is an approach to care the terminal ill patient, not in a specific place like hospital, rather it provides medical services in a home like atmosphere; because at the old age when the patients realize that their time is at the end, they want to die at their home. In fact, in this service, the patients are treated in the home like atmosphere instead of the hospitals. In recent times the concept of old age homes seems to be at par with the Hospice Services. This type of service is, however, widely

EUTHANASIA: A COMPARATIVE STUDY BETWEEN WESTERN AND INDIAN VIEWS

available in the Western countries, whereas in India Hospice Service is limited, because Indian family remains an ideal example at a well-knit social unit. [6]

IV.IV TELLING THE OBVIOUS

Everybody not only wants to lead a meaningful and eventful life, but also favoursa peaceful and dignified death. Most of the developed countries provide the older people pension, insurance on property, security for the spouse, safety measure for the children and the protection for other such worldly matters. It is crucial that all these concerns are properly and adequately be addressed. The doctor may deliver the right information about death to the patient as it is inevitable. After the confirmation of death, the patient can take the steps to complete his or her ongoing works i.e. addressing properly of the said essential components of living for the future generations, within a short period. Meaningful life is nothing but to complete some essential works for the future generation within a stipulated time. If the essential works are done within a short period i.e. the purpose of life is fulfilled, the time of death whether it occurs in a short period or not, is seemed to be unimportant. In the history of human kind, there are many persons who have been living through their works although they have spent a short period in this earth.

EUTHANASIA: A COMPARATIVE STUDY BETWEEN WESTERN AND INDIAN VIEWS

V. EVALUATION

Now we are in a position to make an evaluation of the said other ways for dignifying the death. If Palliative Care is considered, it is observed—it is not affordable for all kind of patients with serious chronic illness. Even in U.S.A, a small percentage of patients who want to be admitted in the Palliative Care centre are failed to get the admission for treatment, due to the shortage of bed. Nearly one-third of United State hospitals do not have any Palliative Care service as well as most of the patients are not well informed about Palliative Care. In 2012, an article, based on a survey, demands, in general, the patients received a palliative consultation38 days before their death.

Now the points are:

Why Palliative Care services have a limited application?

Why the Palliative Care is not accepted by the larger society?

In developed countries, cancer patients are relatively getting comparatively good health care access through Palliative Care units, at least in urban centres. Whereas, in rural areas, the poor patients just get the advice of the specialist through palliative care programs. But the health care professionals should take-care more attention with enough training for the patient who has been searching for Palliative Care. In developing countries, most of rural areas have no sufficient numbers of hospitals. Doctors and some medical students are well known about the importance of Palliative Care, but most of the people are unknown about Palliative Care. Developed counties have failed to construct enoughPalliative Care centres for treatments.

Regarding the life prolonging treatment and hospice service, it can be said that these are too much expensive. Moreover, these two activities are not free from business like attitude.

VI. SOME OTHER WAYS HOW TO DIGNIFY THE DEATH FROM WESTERN PERSPECTIVE

Though *Santhara*, *Sati* or *Jauhar*, *Prayopavesa*, and *Mahasamadhi,* as it has been mentioned earlier, are such type of customs cum activities followed in Indian traditions, may not be treated at par with euthanasia; but these may be taken as the ways through which a person can sacrifice his life in order to dignify his or her death.In case of terminal disease or major disability, a person is free to choose one of these ways to end his or her life. Let it be noted that the Indian sages considered terminal illness, not from absolutely negative aspect as like as an accidental death where the concerned persons are failed to get any moment to think about his or her future. Terminal ill patients, before their death may get sometimesin order to manage his incomplete works after making a thorough discussion with his family members. Finally, the sick patients will die with a peace full mind that he has done his assigned works. Now we are in a position to discusssome of these sacred customs followed by the Indian traditions.

EUTHANASIA: A COMPARATIVE STUDY BETWEEN WESTERN AND INDIAN VIEWS

VI.I SANTHARA

Santhara refers to that type of practice through which the life comes to an end where the gradual reducing of the amount of eating food and taking water is necessary. In the Jain scriptures, it has been recommended as the way to achieve a peaceful and dignified death.Following the Jain tradition, it is believed that it is the manifestation of the attainment of strong self-awareness and spiritual freedomwhen any one firmly welcomes his or her own death through this holy way— *Santhara*which has been practiced since *Rishabhanath*, the founder of Jainism. The practice of *Santhara* has also been recorded as a code of conduct of the Jain sagesin *Pratikraman Sutra* of *ShravakaAnuvrata*. It is learned from this sutra that a Jain sages is permitted to seek for *Santhara*only when all the desires are fulfilled or the body is unable to work anymore due to the routine illness. Let it be noted that the designation of *Santhara* and *Sallekhana* are the same though the term *Santhara*is used by the *Swetambara Jains*, whereas the expression *Sallekhana* is used by the *DigambaraJains*.

According to the Jain scriptures, the practice of *Santhara* can also be followed by any individual person who has been in a good mental state and peaceful mind, but he or she has to undergo the following situations:

I. At the old age when death seems to be imminent.

II. Due to the terminal illness when a person is failed to do his or her normal works.

EUTHANASIA: A COMPARATIVE STUDY BETWEEN WESTERN AND INDIAN VIEWS

III. When a person fulfils all his responsibilities.

After finalizing the decision, before the execution of this practice the concerned person should

a) prepare the mind through a thorough realization of preached scriptures
b) seek permission from the family members and the relatives
c) take apologize from those who have been suffered by his or her wrong doing willingly or unwillingly
d) keep faith on the God as well as in religion

At the time of the execution of *Santhara*, the concerned person is permitted to meditate deeply so that he or she could feel that he or she is thesoul not the body. Through the deep and uninterrupted meditation, he or she can slowly, but gradually restrain himself from food and water to achieve the goal i.e. finally leaving the body.

Recently,in India, a debatable issue has been emerged regarding the legacy of *Santhara*—whether it can be taken as an alternative toeuthanasia where the right to life seems to be dishonoured. Again, some persons fail to distinguish *Santhara* from suicide. The Jain community, however, firmly believes that *Santhara*can never be treated as equal with suicide as there is a clear cut definition and guidance of *Santhara* which has been pointed out earlier. It should not be forgotten thatsuicide is actually, the result of unbalancing mind which is full of anger, anguish andpain. But *Santhara*, being a sacred practice performed by only those who follow the said guidelines where it

EUTHANASIA: A COMPARATIVE STUDY BETWEEN WESTERN AND INDIAN VIEWS

has been clearly mentioned that any kind of force or pressure is prohibited. It is, in fact, meant forgetting salvation.

The debate is based on a case filed by *Gyan* Kumar against the state of Punjab in the Supreme Court as the state of Punjab bans*Santhara* on the ground that it goes against the Article 21 of the Indian constitution where the right to life has been assured, because the right to life is our natural right. As *Santhara* does not bring natural death as like as suicide it is not compatible with the right to life. After justifying all the arguments for and against *Santhara*, the Supreme Court has been convinced that *Santhara* is not at all suicide, but this practiced should not be entertained further as it goes against the Article 21 of the constitution where it is clearly mentioned that the life of any Indian citizen is valuable and the right to die can never be an explanation of the Article 21 of the constitution.

In fact, the concept of right to die and the concept of the *Santhara* are different. The field of the concept of right to die is broader than the field of the concept of *Santhara*. *Santhara* is a kind of religious practice performed by a particular religion. If *Santhara* were granted by the Supreme Court, then there is a chance of misusing it. Anyone, in anytime,may ask for right to die, even a student may file a case in the court for suicide in order to enjoy the right of right to die.

It is not suicide, because the motive of*Santhara* is different from the motive of suicide. Again, *Santhara* is limited to a particular community following the criteria. Only elderly

EUTHANASIA: A COMPARATIVE STUDY BETWEEN WESTERN AND INDIAN VIEWS

persons who have fulfilled all the responsibilities are permitted to choose this practice after a thorough consultation with his or her family. *Santhara* is such kind of activity which dignifies the death, whereas suicide is sudden depending on un-controlling emotions.Suicide is a kind of escape route for the weak persons who are frightened to fight against the ups and downs of life.

Again, *Santhara* cannot be treated at par with euthanasia i.e. mercy killing, because it requires the help a medical practitioner who is fully aware of the current progress of the medical field. The main purpose of euthanasia is to give relieve the patient from unbearable physical pain. After euthanasia, the family members are not permitted to celebrate the occasion, whereas *Santhara* openly accept celebration as it is believed that it leads the concerned person towards the emancipation.

In 2006, *Jaipur* based lawyer Nikhil *Soni* filed a public interest litigation case against *Santhara* in Rajasthan High Court. The bench of High Court said *Santhara* or *Sallekhana*should not be treated as the necessary condition to be emancipated following the Jain scriptures.The high court asked the state not to encourage this practice in any form. If anybody practices*Santhara*, a criminal case must be lodged in accordance with section 309 (attempted suicide) or section 306 (abetment to suicide) of the IPC.[7]

VI.II SATIPRATHA & JAUHAR

The meaning of the word 'sati' has been changed from time to time. The primary meaning of the term 'Sati' was consisted in

EUTHANASIA: A COMPARATIVE STUDY BETWEEN WESTERN AND INDIAN VIEWS

its reference to the goddess Sati who committed self-immolation, because her father *Dakṣa* insulted not only her but also Shiva, her husband. The term 'Sati' is used as a symbol of protest where one does not reluctant to accept death, if he or she is disgraced. So, finally, sati means choosing death with self-respect, rather than a life of humiliation.

The practice of Sati and committing suicide are not same, because their motives are different. The motive of Sati is crystal clear— choosing death with self-respect, rather than a life of humiliation; whereas suicide has different motives.

Subsequently, the purpose of the Sati practice has been changed. During the *Chola* Empire, the Sati practice was aimed at gaining Royal Status where the basic criteria of Sati i.e. the humiliating factor had been given importance. Sacrificing of life for husband was treated as the main factor. Later, when India had been attacked by the Muslims and other foreign powers and defeated, especially the *Rajput* ladies, used to become 'Sati' in order to be escaped from rape, torture and dishonour. Though in the Ramayana, *Mandodari*, the wife of *Ravana*, or the wife of the Bali, did not become 'Sati' after the death of their husband. Rather they got married with their husband's brother, as they were not humiliated. [8]

In fact, Sati was deeply rooted in the Hindu religious system. It was an amalgam of two distinct concepts: religious self-immolation and the burning of widows at their husbands' pyres. [9] Though these concepts are distinct concepts, these

EUTHANASIA: A COMPARATIVE STUDY BETWEEN WESTERN AND INDIAN VIEWS

were common enough among many ancient tribes, and other primitive religious communities. Religious self-immolation is, however, a very important factor. That is why it was observed that in Mahabharata *Madri*decided to jump on the burning pyre of her husband *Pandu,*as she was tremendously influenced by the guilty, she felt in causing the death of her beloved husband. Due to the reverence of Self-immolation and 'death before dishonour principle', the *Rajput* queens used to follow the *Jahar Brata* when their husbands died in the battlefield. And similar social conditions might have induced self-immolation as well as widow burning, in a male-dominated Hindu society, the chastity or purity of Widows became a prominent issue. [10]Let it be noted that some thinkers are in the opinion that chastity is not the sole condition of a woman for practicing Sati. The real problem with the practice of Sati is abuse. What Gandhiji have remarked in this regard is very important. He remarked,

> It is physically impossible to violate a woman against her will. The outrage takes place only when she gives way to fear or does not realize her moral strength. If she cannot meet the assailant's physical might, her purity will give her the strength to die before he succeeds in violating her, for example, *Sita*.[11]

But from present perspective, each and every human being whether he is a man or woman must have the intrinsic value(i.e. right to life per se); and due to the right to life none is permitted to leave his or her life i.e. suicide is also a punishable offence.

EUTHANASIA: A COMPARATIVE STUDY BETWEEN WESTERN AND INDIAN VIEWS

It has been mentioned earlier, the *Jauhar* was practiced by the women when they wanted to keep their dignity from humiliation caused by the foreigners. These women were so conscious about their dignity that they did not left their children in front of unknown future.When there was no chance of winning the war, not only the women used to practice *Jauhar*with their children,but also the defeated soldiers used to sacrifice their life believed in the principle— 'do or die'. For the sake of dignity, when the defeated soldiers used to sacrifice their life, it was called as'*Saka*'. *Kaushik* Ray, the eminent Historian mentionedthat the *Jauhar* practice was implemented only when a Hindu king was attacked by a Muslim invader. [12]

Let us review some historical *Jauhar* practices by the *Rajput* at *Chittaur* fort in Rajasthan.

In the year 1103, *AlauddinKhilji*, the Sultan of Delhi as well as the founder of *Khilji*Dynastyheardabout the dazzling beauty of *Padmini*, the wife of *RanaBhim* Singh of *Chittaur*and decided to attack at once in order to be the sole possessor of that beautiful queen. *Rana Bhim* Singh with his trained and brave army fought valiantly against the Sultan but was defeated. When *Padmini* got this sad news, she with the other women and children along with the valuable designed ornament jumped into the fire in order to keep their dignity.[13]

Same situation occurred in 1535 A.D. when *Chittaur* was attacked by the Sultan *Bahadur* of *Gujrat*. At that time *RanaVikramjit* was the king of *Mewar*. Near about 13000 women and children sacrificed their lives after jumping over the fire for honour. [14]

Finally, in 1568when *Uday* Singh, the king of *Chittaur* was attacked by Akbar, the *Badsa* of Delhi the last notable *Jauhar* practiced was performed as the *Rajput* warriors were defeated after fighting their best. Countless mother, sisters, daughters, and wives of warriors have sacrificed their lives for self-respect and dignity. [15]

VI.III PRAYOPAVESASA

Following Hinduism,*Prayopavesa* means fasting till the death. A person, from religious perspective, may decide to go for *Prayopavesa*when he is at the verge of death due to the age or routine illness through a public announcement. *Prayopavesa* must be public, in order to differentiate it from suicide, in the one hand and from assisted suicide on the other. Before the execution of *Prayopavesa*, the family members can settle any dispute related to the wealth of the concerned person with the help of an attorney so that none can blame anyone. The attorney can clarify the motive of the patient for selecting *Prayopavesa*following the health care guide lines as prescribed by the physicians. The concerned person may take apologize for his wrong deedsafter a thorough self evaluation about his performed actions in his whole life and concentrate on the scriptures as well as the teachings of the Guru. When the concerned person realizes that he is actually the soul not the body after a deep and prolonged meditation, he may leave his life abstaining from food.

In the *BhāgavataPurāna*, we see that king *Parikshit*left his own life following *Prayopavesa*. *Vinayak Damodar Savarkar*, in recent time, departed through *Prayopavesa*. In 1982,*Acharya BinobaBhabe*and in 2001, *SatguruSivayaSubramuniaswami*also went to the peace heaven following *Prayopavesa*. Thus from ancient times to modern times, *Prayopavesa* hasbeen practiced. Ancient thinkers were aware of the dignity of the individual from the perspective of living as well as from the aspect of death.

VI.IV MAHASAMADHI

The word *Mahasamadhi* is used to describe the final exit of the soul of a Yogi from the body. It is too hard to understand for the ordinary people. It is, an art which is performed consciously as well as intentionally when a Yogi left his body. This is actually the result of constant spiritual enlightenment of the Yogi. From the perspective of Hindu or Yogic tradition,*Mahasamadhi*means when a Yogi is in a state of deep meditation i.e. the achievement of the final state of Samadhiwhere the soul unites with the universal soul as like as the doll made of salt melted in the saline water[16]through an uninterrupted constant practice. As there is no life after the *Mahasamadhi*, it is known as Para *Mukti* or *Nirvikalpa* Samadhi which enables a person to be free from the cycle of karma.

Achievement of the *Mahasamadhi* of *ParamhansaYogananda*has been noted down by *Daya* Mata, one

EUTHANASIA: A COMPARATIVE STUDY BETWEEN WESTERN AND INDIAN VIEWS

of the ardent disciples of *Yogananda* in the book— 'Finding the joy within.' Before the attainment of *Mahasamadhi*, *Yogananda*announced he would leave the world within few hours and he wanted to have a walk. Finally, the eyes of *Yogananda* took positionin the middle of the eye brow which is called *kuthastha* Kendra and he stopped his breathing on March 7th, 1952 after uttering, "where Ganges, Woods, Himalayan caves, and men dream God, I am hallowed, my body touched that sod." [17]In the same way, *ShyamacharanLahiriMahasaya* also achieved in the state of *Mahasamadhi* on 26thSeptember 1895.

VIII. CONCLUSION

From the discussion mentioned above it is clear, following Indian perspective, death was not just passing away at least for the Yogi(s). After leading an event full life in the earth, due to the spiritual power caused by uninterrupted practice of deepmeditation, the Yogi(s) used to assume the exact time of the*Mahasamadhi*. Whereas, the general human beings are unable to understand what power they have as they have too much attachment on the material world. From this, one should not draw the conclusion that only the Yogi(s) are liable to make their death dignified. A purely household person may be allowed to dignify his death, if he or she follows the spiritual path after concentrating his or her mind in the lotus feet of the almighty God.

EUTHANASIA: A COMPARATIVE STUDY BETWEEN WESTERN AND INDIAN VIEWS

Notes & References:

1. Kumar, Dr. Adarsh, Thejaswi, H.T., Gupta, S.K.: *Present Status of Euthanasia in India from Medico-legal perspective an update* in *Journal of Punjub Academic of Forensic Medicine and Toxicology*, Vol. 14, Issue.1, January 2014, pp.59-64

2. Humphry, D. (Ed.): *The Practicalities of Self-Deliverance and Assisted Suicide for the dying*, Time Books International, New Delhi, 1991

3. Terminal care for the elderly, therefore, aims to provide relief from frequent physical pain, to assure a degree of hope and—possibly—to prolong life. — From Chatterjee, ChoraSuhita., Patnaik, Priyadarshi., Chariar, Vijayraghaban. M. (Ed.): *Discourses on Aging and Dying*, SAGE publications India Pvt. Ltd, 2008, P-219

4. Eutsey, D.E.(Ed.): *Patients and Family Issues, Palliative Care: Patient and Family Counselling Manual*, MD: Aspen Publishers Inc., Gaithersberg, 1996

5. Chatterjee, ChoraSuhita., Patnaik, Priyadarshi., Chariar, Vijayraghaban. M. (Ed.): *Discourses on Aging and Dying*, SAGE publications India Pvt. Ltd, 2008, P-221

6. Basham, A.L.: Aspects of Ancient Indian Culture, Asia Publishing House, New York, 1970

7. Sethi, Dr. Rajesh: *Euthanasia: Legalising Euthanasia In India, A survey of Attitude of Doctors, Lawyers and Academics in an urban setting*, civil daily.com, indiatvnews.com, legal service India.com

8. Gilmartin, Sophie: *The Sati, the Bride and the Widow: Sacrificial Woman in the Nineteenth Century*, Victorian Literature and Culture, Cambridge University Press, Vol. 25, Issue No. 1, 1997, P-141

9. Ganeri, Jonardon(Ed.): *The Collected Essays of Bimal Krishna Matilal Ethics and Epics*, Oxford University Press, New Delhi, 2002, P-154

10. Gilmartin, Sophie: *The Sati, the Bride, and the Widow: Sacrificial Woman in the Nineteenth Century*, in Victorian Literature and Culture, Cambridge University Press, Vol. 25, No. 1, 1997, P—141

11. *Harijan*, 14th January 1940

EUTHANASIA: A COMPARATIVE STUDY BETWEEN WESTERN AND INDIAN VIEWS

12. Roy, Kaushik: *Hinduism and the Ethics of Warfare in South Asia: From Antiquity to the Present,* Cambridge University Press, London, 2012, pp. 182-184

13. Thomas, Catherine Weinberger: *Ashes of Immortality: Widow-Burning in India,* University of Chicago Press. Chicago, 1999, pp. 121–123

14. Jenkins ,Everett Jr.: *The Muslim Diaspora A Comprehensive Chronology of the Spread of Islam in Asia, Africa, Europe and the Americas, Volume 2,* McFarland, 2000, P-58

15. Narayan, Uma: *Dislocating Cultures: Identities, Traditions, and Third World Feminism,* Routledge, London, 1997, pp. 59–65

16. Gupta Mahendranath: *Sri Sri Ramakrishna Kathamrita Volume 1,* (A son of the Lord and Disciple), Calcutta, 1902, P-104

17. Sushila, Blackman: *Graceful Exits: How Great Beings Die: Death Stories of Tibetan, Hindu & Zen Masters.* New York, 1997

I heard a lot about the idea of dying "with dignity" while my mother was sick. It was only near her very end that I gave much thought to what this idea meant. I didn't actually feel it was undignified for my mother's body to fail—that was the human condition. Having to help my mother on and off the toilet was difficult, but it was natural. The real indignity, it seemed, was dying where no one cared for you the way your family did, dying where it was hard for your whole family to be with you and where excessive measures might be taken to keep you alive past a moment that called for letting go. I didn't want that for my mother. I wanted her to be able to go home. I didn't want to pretend she wasn't going to die. — Meghan O'Rourke, An American writer, poet and critic

CHAPTER: 5

Conclusion

EUTHANASIA: A COMPARATIVE STUDY BETWEEN WESTERN AND INDIAN VIEWS

CHAPTER: 5

Conclusion

Only two kinds of people can attain self-knowledge: those who are not encumbered at all with learning, that is to say, whose minds are not over crowded with thoughts borrowed from others; and those who, after studying all the scriptures and sciences, have come to realise that they know nothing.—Sri Ramakrishna Paramhansa

I. INTRODUCTION

On the basis of the discussed **CHAPTER—I: INTRODUCTION, CHAPTER—II: EUTHANASIA AND ITS TYPES, CHAPTER—III:LIMITATIONS OF EUTHANASIA,** and **CHAPTER—IV:SOME OTHER THEORIES AND THEIR LIMITATIONS** now, we are in a position to draw the conclusion of this research work. Formerly, it has been talked about for more than one time, that one should not be assumed this research work is concerned only with a mere comparative study between Western and Indian concept of euthanasia, from the title of the research work: **EUTHANASIA: A COMPARATIVE STUDY BETWEEN WESTERN AND INDIAN VIEWS**. In fact, the prime objective of this research work is to find out a way, on the basis of the comparative study between Western and Indian concept of euthanasia, through which the death can be dignified, especially, for those who have been suffering from terminal illness i.e. an incurable disease that cannot be adequately treated and is reasonably expected to result to death.

EUTHANASIA: A COMPARATIVE STUDY BETWEEN WESTERN AND INDIAN VIEWS

From 17th Century and it's onwards, intellectual tradition in the West has been tremendously influenced by the dualistic theory propounded by Rene Descartes. Following mind body dualism, it is said that human beings are comprised of two distinct substances—body and mind or soul. Body, being extended and mind, being conscious are opposite to each other and categorically different.Bodily activities are public, whereas the activities of mind, is totally private.[1]Later on, however, this theory i.e. the mind dualism of Descartes has been familiarized as the 'Official Doctrine of Mind'and it has been logically dismissed by Gylebert Ryle on the basis of 'category mistake'.[2]Wittgenstein, however, considered mind as a 'beetle in a beetle box' which can never be observed by other except oneself and we should not give much attention on the analysis of the meaning of the mindas we all know how to use the term mind in a particular language following a specific'language game'.[3]Recently, some philosophers hold that mind is nothing but the function of brain. As a result, the concept of death has been started to be rested upon mechanistic analogies, and is, therefore, death is considered as being opposition of life. It happens when the body-machines packs up, thus, somehow generating the idea that the process can be controlled through scientific intervention. Both aging and dying are looked at form a disease perspective and as these are obstacles, these are to be overcome. This perspective governs end-of-life care as well, resulting in excessive medicalization of death.

EUTHANASIA: A COMPARATIVE STUDY BETWEEN WESTERN AND INDIAN VIEWS

Naturally, this Western attitude of death, has made a little success in achieving a meaningful place of the central issue of the thesis: how the death will be meaningful and/or dignified as like as life? Rather controversies arise in the field of death including the question how death should be dignified as well as the appropriate treatments for the aged. Debates have also been surfaced about how much resources need to be directed for unlimited life extension, the degrees of controlling the measurements of the health of the aged. Euthanasia, physician assisted suicide, palliative care, life-prolonged treatment, hospice service and telling the obvious are also not free from criticism.

II. A BRIEF RESUME OF THE EARLIER CHAPTERS

However, before entering into the detail measurement of, how far, this work has been successfully made an advance progress; in order to achieve the aim of this research work, let us resume in a very brief what have been discussed in the previous chapters.

CH. NO.	NAME	ABRIDGED SUBJECT MATTER
01	Introduction	In this introductory chapter, the associate concepts, fundamentals, research issue, purpose, research methodology and the delimitation of this research work has been discussed. In fact, this chapter acts as the road map of the entire research work. At the outset, the definition of death, different types of death, issues and theories related to death have been analysed. Euthanasia, is, however, mainly related to the death of terminal ill persons. From the Western

EUTHANASIA: A COMPARATIVE STUDY BETWEEN WESTERN AND INDIAN VIEWS

		perspective, euthanasia, being too much mechanical, fails to keep intact the dignity of death though each and every entity whether it is animate or inanimate of this planet has an intrinsic value. Human species, being the top, must be the subject of this intrinsic value. Even the death should be dignified whether it is caused by the terminal illness or by normally. If the Indian perspective is considered, though euthanasia has not been used in literal sense in Indian context, it may help the terminal ill patients to give a dignified death. But how is this possible? This research work is meant for making an intensive query through a morphological cum analytical study to justify the answer of this question.
02	Euthanasia & It's type	This chapter aims to amplify the place of euthanasia in the history of medical ethics from ancient time to modern time by making a brief sketch of (i) the concept of euthanasia, (ii) its relation to other types of death, (iii) different kinds of euthanasia and its justification (iv) detail analysis of the moral preference of active and passive euthanasia and (v) different types of euthanasia like socio-religious activities in India.
		Euthanasia, a kind of easy and gentle death, especially for the terminal ill patient are three kinds—a) voluntary b) involuntary and c) non– voluntary. Voluntary euthanasia: voluntary euthanasia can be defined as a means chosen by a patient by making a request Involuntary euthanasia: involuntary euthanasia refers to that situation where euthanasia occurs in spite of the objection of a patient or his surrogate

EUTHANASIA: A COMPARATIVE STUDY BETWEEN WESTERN AND INDIAN VIEWS

		Non-voluntary euthanasia: It occurs without the fully informed consent and request of an adult patient competent to take decision or that of his surrogates
		Among the active or passive euthanasia, which is morally acceptable? A debate put forwarded by James Rachels, has been analysed. Furthermore, in Indian part, *Santhara, Sati* or *Jauhar, Prayopavesa*, and *Mahasamadhi*are also discussed as the euthanasia like activities in order to coverboth the Western and Indian viewpoints regarding euthanasia.
03	Limitations of Euthanasia	This chapter has focused on a detail analysis of the arguments for and against of Euthanasiaby using two types of arguments—Effective Evidence Arguments and Arguments from Case Study, as it is concerned with the taking the life of the self conscious human being. Among the Effective Evidence Arguments for euthanasia, Arguments based MEDICAL GROUND, THE DIGNITY OF LIFE, RIGHT TO DIE, REFUSING ANY MEDICAL TREATMENT, EQUAL IMPORTANCE ON RIGHT TO LIFE AND DEATH, PROTECTION OF LIFE, DUTY TO RELIEF FROM MISERY, OBSERVATION OF THE OPINION OF DESMOD TUTU, ARGUMENT PUT FORWARDED BY MICHEL IRWIN, ARGUMENT OF STEPHEN HAWKING, ARGUMENT BY MARICA ANGELLandARGUMENT OF JACKSON KEVORKIANare important.On the other hand,Argument of Case Study are rested upon the consecutive case studies made by David Goodall, an Australian botanist and ecologist; Annette Childs, a psychotherapist;Jerry Brown, the Governor of California and Brittany Maynard, a 29-year old woman who had been suffering with stage 4 *Glioblastoma multiforme* (a malignant brain tumour).Among the arguments which are

EUTHANASIA: A COMPARATIVE STUDY BETWEEN WESTERN AND INDIAN VIEWS

		put forwarded against euthanasia, THE RELIGIOUS ARGUMENT, THE SLIPPERY SLOPE ARGUMENT, MEDICAL ETHICS ARGUMENT, ALTERNATIVE ARUMENT, ARGUMENT FROM LEGALIZATION, ARGUMENT FROM THE CONFLICT INTEREST, ARGUMENT FROM THE CARE, ARGUMENT OF PROFESSION, ARGUMENT FROM THE BURDEN TO SOCIETY and ARGUMENT OF NON-REPLACE-ABILITY are important. From the analysis of the arguments for and against Euthanasia, it is clear that Euthanasia, being a public health policy goes ahead of time. It is morally permissible, but its legalization depends on the enlightenment of the entire human species.
04	Some other theories and their Limitations	This chapter deals with the theories which are other than different types of euthanasia. Among these, Palliative Care, Life prolonging treatment, Hospice Services and Telling the obvious truth are from Western perspective which are linked with the fundamental question of this research work i.e. how death can be dignified? From the Indian perspective, *Santhara, Sati* or *Jauhar, Prayopavesa,* and *Mahasamadhi* arediscuused amongst which *Santhara, Prayopavesa,* and *Mahasamadhi* are seems to be fundamental and closely related to the answer of the research question.

III. FINAL CONCLUSION

From this background, if euthanasia is reconsidered again; it is observed that it is yet to be accepted as public health policy by most of the countries of this world. In fact, the arguments for and against, seems to carry the same weight. From the perspective of freedom of choice, dignity of life, limitations of human resources and social responsibilities, euthanasia seems

EUTHANASIA: A COMPARATIVE STUDY BETWEEN WESTERN AND INDIAN VIEWS

to be granted as a public health policy. On the other hand, from the perspective of professional responsibilities of the medical persons, wishes of the nearest and dearest,theology, and the feasibilities of the implementation, euthanasia seems to be banned.A young person, who has been suffering from the incurable disease, is free to consider the euthanasia. But the crucial point is: in this highly modern technological era there are no fixed criteria through which a disease could be announced as incurable. However, euthanasia may be entertained for those who are aged;have already done their assigned duties, as well as very much conscious about what is euthanasia.

Now, the point is: whether the death is dignified by the euthanasia or not. As the consideration of euthanasia, still now,is a debatable issue for the self conscious human being; it can never bring directlythe dignity of death for a person who has been suffering from terminal illness or not. If the other policies such as palliative care,life prolonging treatments, hospice services, telling the obvious are considered,following the Western perspective, what is true—these are too much mechanical.A mechanical attitude may be hundred percent logical, but it devoid of any human values. Each and every individual of this planet must have some values—instrumental and intrinsic. Even death should be dignified whether it is caused by the terminal illness or by normally. These Western polices being mechanical, have failed to cover this point. Moreover, euthanasia, palliative care, life prolonging treatment

EUTHANASIA: A COMPARATIVE STUDY BETWEEN WESTERN AND INDIAN VIEWS

and hospice service are not free from business like attitude. However, from purely materialistic perspective, in future,euthanasia may be considered legally as well as morally for the sake of future generation. But the consideration of euthanasia and dignifying the death are not the same, though it is true that all self conscious human being expect that his or her death must be dignified as like as his or her life. That is why it seems that materialistic attitude is not sufficient condition, though it may be a necessary condition of dignifying the death. It is a necessary condition in this sense that the concerned person himself or herself wills for his or her own death.

If the Indian perspective is considered, though euthanasia has not been used in literal sense, it may help the terminal ill patients to give a dignified death. But the point is: how? Before clarifying the answer of the point, let us revisit the Indian standpoint regarding the implementation of euthanasia. When a twenty-five years old young man of Andhra named K. *Venkatesh*, in December 2004, wanted to execute the power of right to death so that he could donate some of his vital organs before his death for others, through a plea made by his mother to the Andhra Pradesh High Court; it has been observed that his last will has not been entertained by the court. Being the true follower of ahimsa, Mahatma Gandhi also favoured euthanasia on the ground of medical emergency. His argument is like this: if a doctor is permissible to operate any malfunctioning organ for the betterment of future, euthanasia may be permissible under certain imperative circumstances. It has been mentioned

EUTHANASIA: A COMPARATIVE STUDY BETWEEN WESTERN AND INDIAN VIEWS

earlier (CHAPTER IV, POINT 2. BACKGROUND OF THE LEGAL IMPLEMENTATION OF PASSIVE EUTHANASIA IN INDIA)that passive euthanasia i.e. by means of withdrawal of life support where a patient has been in a permanent vegetative state is not illegal in India on and from 7th March, 2011 following the verdict of Supreme Court of India after a case filled by *PinkiVirani* for *Aruna Shanbaug.*In fact, it is a landmark of Indian stand point towards euthanasia. That is why *Prashant Bhushan,* a senior Supreme Court lawyer commented on *Aruna Shanbaug* as:

> ...the right to live is the right to live with dignity. If you can't live with dignity, life really has no meaning. If you are forced to live a life of indignity or great suffering, then that clearly violates your right to life.[4]

From the above discussion, for the Indians, it is clear that there is a close connection, at least in an underlying manner, between euthanasia and the dignity of death. Though in India, from the Vedic age, there are many examples of suicides committed on religious grounds. In the Mahabharata and the Ramayana we find many instances of religious suicides. But most of the Hindus would not accept euthanasia on the request of the patient as the Hindus do not believe the separation of the soul from the body at an unnatural time, because euthanasia causes the soul departed from body at an unnatural time. If the soul departs from the body at an unnatural time then the law of Karma is violated. Again, euthanasia cannot be permitted on the ground that it opposes the teaching of ahimsa. However, there are some cases where helping to end a painful life of a person

EUTHANASIA: A COMPARATIVE STUDY BETWEEN WESTERN AND INDIAN VIEWS

has not been rejected only when it has been performed following the religious background, because in that case the death of a person is dignified. Govardana and Kulluka, at the time of writing commentaries on Manu, remarked a man may carry out the *mahaprastha* (great departure) i.e. the journey towards the end of life when he has been either suffering from incurably diseased or have met with a great misfortune.[5] In fact, the Western tradition, being mechanical seems to be failed to disclose this particular point, whereas, Indians are habituated to recommend each individual soul is immortal by nature and continues to exist even after the death of the body.[6] Indic view does not show much care about the body ailment. It emphasizes on the honour of the spirit as well as the salvation of soul. That's why *Sati* or *Jauhar* has been performed by the *Rajput* ladies for their dignity of life, whereas, *Santhara, Prayopavesa,* and *Mahasamadhi* have been performed for the dignity of soul.

Notes &References:

1. And although I may, or rather, as I will shortly say, although I certainly do possess a body with which I am very closely conjoined; nevertheless, because, on the one hand, I have a clear and distinct idea of myself, in as far as I am only a thinking and unextended thing, and as, on the other hand, I possess a distinct idea of body, in as far as it is only an extended and unthinking thing, it is certain that I, [that is, my mind, by which I am what I am], is entirely and truly distinct from my body, and may exist without it. From Haldane, Elizabeth S.(Tr.): ReneDescartes's*Meditations of First Philosophy*, Cambridge University Press, 1911

2. One of the chief intellectual origins of what I have yet to prove to be the Cartesian category-mistake seems to be this. When Galileo showed that his methods of scientific discovery were competent to provide a mechanical theory which should cover every occupant of space, Descartes found in him-self two

EUTHANASIA: A COMPARATIVE STUDY BETWEEN WESTERN AND INDIAN VIEWS

conflicting motives. As a man of scientific genius he could not but endorse the claims of mechanics, yet as a religious and moral man he could not accept, as Hobbes accepted, the discouraging rider to those claims, namely that human nature differs only in degree of complexity from clockwork. The mental could not be just a variety of the mechanical. From Ryle, Gilbert: *The Concept of Mind*, Routledge, London, 1949, P—8

3. No one can look into anyone else's box, and everyone says he knows what a beetle is only by looking at his beetle. —Here it would be quite possible for everyone to have something different in his box. One might even imagine such a thing constantly changing.—But suppose the word "beetle" had a use in these people's language?—If so it would not be used as the name of a thing. The thing in the box has no place in the language-game at all; not even as a something: for the box might even be empty.—No, one can 'divide through' by the thing in the box; it cancels out, whatever it is. From Anscombe, G.E.(Tr.)Ludwig Wittgenstein's *Philosophical Investigation*, Basil Blackwell, Oxford, 1953, P-100

4. Sara, Sally:*India's Supreme Court Considers Euthanasia Application*, The World Today, 18thDecember 2009, <http://www.abc.net.au/worldtoday/content/2009/s2775801.htm> accessed 19thNovember 2020.

5. Bhhler, George (Tr.): *Laws of Manu, Sacred Books of the East by F. Maxmuller*, Vol. 25, 1967, P– 206

6. *yaenaṁ vettihantāraṁ yaścainaṁ manyatehatam |*

   ubhau tau navijānītonāyaṁhantinahanyate ||

One who deems the Self a slayer, and one who thinks of it as slain — both are ignorant; for the Self neither slays nor is slain. (*Verse 19, Chapter II of the Gitā*)

> The pessimist sees difficulty in every opportunity. The optimist sees opportunity in every difficulty. Winston Churchill

CPSIA information can be obtained
at www.ICGtesting.com
Printed in the USA
BVHW032038151022
649470BV00014B/1039

9 782214 153765